1

RIVER STONES GROW PLANTS

2018 EDITION

By

RICHARD C. CAMPBELL

Contributions by:

Dr. H. Henry Teng, Dept. of Chemistry, Geology Program; Environmental Resource Policy Program - The George Washington University

Arvazena (Zena) Clardy, Ph.D. Assistant Professor of Horticulture, 4-H SET and NRCS Outreach - Tennessee State University

Published by

Cardinal Publishing

Imprint: To Soil Less

Contributions from Dr. Zena Clardy and Dr. Henry Teng

Chief Editor: Matt Brann.

Edited by Yola Balde, Gwendolyn Johnson, Uncle Logan, Joanne Maldonado, Leila Campbell and David Roach.

Cover Graphics by Rodney Herring

Photography by Richard Campbell

To Soil Less website by GreenLightDesignStudios.com

Table of Contents

Author's Note

Each year we issue a new edition in the study of geological agriculture or gravel gardening. This years' 7th edition includes academic contributions from George Washington University (GWU) and Tennessee State University (TSU). Professors at GWU examined geological characteristics, while professors and students at TSU assessed baseline agriculture aspects of geological farming. These studies begin to shape the academic building blocks of this new science. New to this edition is the business of geological agriculture section, which outlines 17 business sub-industries of geological agriculture. This edition includes a 33-page gravel gardening gallery of the past few years along with the geological agriculture glossary of terms, sharing an overview of new terms to describe the process of the rock-based crop sustainment.

It has been a fulfilling yet challenging journey seeking to bring to reality the notion that rocks can produce crops; getting life out of something thought dead. For now, I refer to myself as Pheidippides of ancient Greece, who is the central figure in the story of the marathon. He is said to have run the 26 miles from Marathon to Athens to deliver news of a military victory against the Persians. Like Pheidippides, I find myself running to tell the news that rocks can grow crops. Since this is still a relative secret in a society of news untold, my journey is not over. Soon, however, my run should become easier as society begins to embrace the notion of geological agriculture.

I would like to thank my family who supported me through this process including Russell Campbell Sr., Leila Campbell, Russell Campbell Jr., Gregory Campbell, Dianna Campbell, Sheranda Campbell, Logan Campbell and Sylvia Campbell. I mainly express gratitude to the Logans for their support and experimentation. Had uncle Logan not posed the question back in 1994, "Richard how is this possible?" the modern-day study of geological agriculture may not have been born.

Much of the elementary school content and photos in this book is due to Lowell School of Washington, DC, whose staff have been excellent stewards and pioneers, accepting gravel gardening early. Special thanks to Debbie Gibbs, Wendy McGrath, Lisa Alfonso-Frank, Stefania Rubino, Katie Wakana, Carolyn B. Law, Leslie Sinsay, Denielle Hill and the entire pre-primary staff. I would also like to thank Audrey Dassignies and Andrew Stanoch and the students of the garden club at Yu Ying Charter School for pioneering the gravel grow cups in an elementary school environment.

A special thank you goes out to all of the homeowners, schools and retailers whose gravel gardens or gravel grow cups are photographed in this book, including Steve and Erica Oliver, Laura Howard, uncle Logan, Lowell School, Yu Ying Public Charter School, Old Takoma Ace Hardware of Takoma Park, MD, David Roach, Leroy Williams, Laura Howard and the Oakland Beautification Society. We are grateful for the efforts of my wife, Sheranda Campbell, and my son, Logan, and daughter, Sylvia, for their day-to-day suffering of rocks around the house. Special thanks to Dr. Anthony LaBude, Larry Harbin, Gwen Wunderlich, Jessica Penzari, Jamal Pope, Clint Albin, Jama Jibrell, Yola Balde, Gwendolyn Johnson, Rogers Gilliard, Lee Williams, Dr. Edwin Nichols and Madeline Ramos for being an excellent research and marketing team.

On the back cover in fine print, you may notice the phrase, "Make the workmanship surpass the materials" by Ovid, a Roman poet. My mentor and uncle Logan, said this to me at the completion of this book. But his statement is meant more for you than me. To rephrase, the material is gravel or basic river rocks; what you do with them is what matters. The workmanship with gravel to produce food surpasses the gravel itself. Simply put, make gravel gardening surpass the gravel.

As a young science, much is to be discovered, revealed and fine-tuned with geological agriculture. As an individual, I can only take this new science and all it has to offer so far. At some point, geological agriculture should take on a life of its own and society can take a step closer towards food security. We applaud all those who have been courageous enough to take a second look at rocks. If rocks + seeds + water = plants, what does this mean for world hunger?

Finally, we say thank you to the creator of the Earth for providing the resources for food security both on land and in the seas. God created the Earth rich with minerals for sustainment. Man did not create the rocks of the sea; we just figured out how to use them for other purposes.

This 7th edition includes everything we know so far about geological agriculture. We hope you find it useful. Good luck and enjoy.

Chapter 1
Gravel Gardening Fundamentals

It is important to review this entire manual before starting the construction and assembly of your indoor or outdoor gravel garden. A proper review of the manual will prevent any missteps from occurring that can or will result in no growth when not following certain procedures. All images taken in this book are of plants grown in gravel except where noted.

Welcome

Welcome to the world of geological agriculture - your first step in alternative gardening 2.0; gravel gardening. This guide will outline the steps necessary to incorporate gravel gardening techniques and practices into your home and growing environments. You will learn 1) the basics and the science behind gravel-based agriculture, 2) materials required, and 3) various applications and management techniques. Once you assemble your gravel garden correctly, you should not have to change nor replace the gravel for years, while still producing crops annually.

Geological agriculture is the process of growing plants in an all-rock or gravel environment absent of soil and fertilizers. Also known as geo-ag or gravel gardening, this method of cultivating crops enables plants to complete a full growing cycle from germination to harvest in river stones. The study of geological agriculture is in its infancy and was discovered by accident in 1994 by uncle Logan and accidental scientist Richard Campbell when uncle Logan asked Campbell why there was a watermelon growing in a rock bed outdoors. Campbell hypothesized that rocks likely are providing nutrients for the watermelon. Campbell asserted that rocks are minerals and minerals are also nutrients and that nutrients are also sometimes vitamins. Certain rocks and fertilizers are likely cousins, concluded Campbell. This notion led uncle Logan to try other seed types, planting additional seeds in his gravel bed and watching more and more plants grow each year. In 2010, uncle Logan asked Campbell two questions: 1) With the growth that we see in gravel, can you figure out what is going on / why this works? and 2) can you share this with the greater society once determined? With Campbell's mother and uncle Logan's wife as witnesses to the conversation, Campbell agreed, and the study of geological agriculture was born.

To Soil Less™ was founded by Campbell in 2010 to research the attributes of rocks as a fertilizing source and to share this approach to crop cultivation with society. Campbell's research uncovered that sedimentary rock has nutrient organic matter within the formation of the rock itself capable of supporting plant life. Given that his research also revealed that modern science views this as an impossibility, Campbell coined the term geological agriculture and began developing new definitions and a lexicon around explaining the process. The foundation of the science centers on the Campbell Equation, which posits that Water + River Rock = Nutrient Materials. By 2016, Campbell was awarded the patent to geological agriculture, and in 2017 Cardinal Publishing decided to disseminate Campbell's work.

Periodically Campbell produces and posts on his website (www.tosoilless.com) the annual edition on geological agriculture called *Grown in Gravel: The Study of Geological Agriculture*. In this 2018 version, the name of the edition has changed to *Rivers Stones Grow Plants*. The 2018 edition includes contributions from the Tennessee State University School of Agriculture and the George Washington University School of Applied Sciences along with observations conducted at Lowell School and Yu Ying Elementary School in Washington, DC, as well as, growing activity at Ace Hardware in Takoma Park, MD, and from various participating homeowners.

Gravel Gardening Benefits

There are several benefits to adopting gravel gardening techniques including but not limited to the following:

1. **Reduced Soil Use** – When you go gravel, you no longer need to use soil to grow many types of plants. You can mix soil with gravel if you choose, but gravel by itself can cultivate crops.

2. **Less Watering** – Proper construction requires a semi-enclosed environment where water is stored longer in the gravel ecosystem than in soil settings. Consequently, outdoor gravel gardens use over 50% less water.

3. **Reduced Reliance on Fertilizers** – The gravel itself provides the basic nutrient materials to sustain plant growth. The cultivation process with gravel does not require man-made artificial fertilizers.

4. **Less Weeding** – Proper construction requires several layers of plastic and lawn fabric underneath the gravel. The barriers of lawn fabric and plastic prevent soil-based weeds from growing in the gravel garden. Consequently, gravel gardens reduce the need for weeding and nearly eliminates the need for weeding products. Airborne weeds will still land on the gravel and can grow.

5. **Cultivation Degradation** – Crop production degrades the nutrient value of the soil, causing the need for fertilizers and/or crop rotation. With gravel, after each harvest, the remaining leaves and vines decompose and decay back into the gravel bed, enhancing the growing environment each year instead of degrading it.

6. **All Natural** – The primary ingredients of gravel gardens are river pea gravel, sand and cotton, which are all-natural materials.

7. **Less Cost** – Once you set up your gravel garden, it can last 20+ years without the need for more gravel and sand, while producing crops each year. The cost of a bag of gravel is the same or less than a bag of soil. By reducing the need to buy fertilizers and weed-and-feed chemicals, you spend less.

8. **Drought Resistant** – With proper construction, if the outdoor temperature rises to 100+ degrees, the underbelly of the garden should remain 75 to 80 degrees on the inside. The temperature contrast creates condensation within the gravel, allowing the rocks to sweat and thus creating moisture.

9. **Organic** – Farmers and commercial growers can adopt principals of gravel gardening to improve the chances of attaining certified organic status.

10. **Nutrient Value** – When testing the nutrient value of crops grown in gravel, the results have shown that gravel-grown cucumbers have the same if not better nutritional value as soil-grown plants.

These benefits of gravel gardening provide practitioners an array of opportunities to make the agricultural process more efficient. The rest of this book provides the necessary information to construct and maintain a successful gravel garden growing environment.

Gravel Gardening Limitations

Despite the numerous benefits, geological agriculture techniques do come with some limitations. General observations uncovered a variety of apparent limitations but do not delve into actual problem-solving techniques on how to overcome observed limitations. Limitations are shared early to guide readers to manage expectations of this evolving science. There are several currently identified weaknesses to adopting gravel gardening techniques including but not limited to the following:

1. **Plant Variety Limitations** – Some plants do better than others in gravel so there will be times when favorite plants like oregano or lavender may not grow in gravel.

2. **Weather** – Soil tends to have a wider range of supporting plant life in temperatures as low as 35 degrees, where gravel tends to slow down at 50 degrees. An outdoor gravel growing environment is only 3 to 4 inches deep, so adverse cold temperatures will kill roots faster than the roots that are 3 to 4 feet deep in the soil.

3. **Deep-Rooted Plants** – Since most outdoor gravel gardens are 3 to 4 inches deep, the environment is not suited for carrots and other deep rooted plants. In this book, however, we do provide samples of some deep-rooted plants such as sweet potatoes and onions.

4. **Retail-ability** – There are several retail products related to gravel gardening but the produced grown in gravel is not necessarily one of them. Some plants, like the seeds from a gravel-grown sunflower, can last through a retail cycle, but generally speaking, crops grown in gravel are designed for consumption the same day or within a few days. Gravel-grown plants are not that resilient once picked, lasting only a few days. Additional research will need to provide clarity on the resiliency of gravel-grown crops.

5. **Irregular Growth** – Some plants grow somewhat irregular in gravel such as begonias, basil, and hyacinth. Currently, the rationale explaining why string beans grow an inch per day in gravel, but basil will grow but very small is unknown. This book provides a list of plants that tend to do well in gravel gardens.

6. **Old Seeds** – As with common soil, seed quality makes a difference in production quality. Current year seeds tend to grow better in gravel than seeds from prior years.

7. **Falling Pots** – Gravel growing areas assembled in pots, cups or any portable container run the risk of falling plants. When plants fall in gravel, the hardness of the rocks will bruise and often kill the softer roots.

8. **Industry Experts** – The single biggest limitation with geological agriculture is that agriculture industry experts cannot seem to understand how this is possible. Each of the major institutions is aware of the claims, but since they do not have a person on the staff that can back up the claims they tend to scoff at the idea. With no global data of this approach, industry experts are generally left baffled, opting to hold for the moment.

Soil Limitations

The soil, on the other hand, is the cornerstone of gardening and agriculture, but it comes with several key challenges, including but not limited to the following:

1. **Soil Degradation** – Every year crops grow means a reduction in the amount of nutrients within soil. Continuous cultivation can reduce soil productivity, yielding fallow seasons, requiring crop rotation, cover cropping, and other supplements to upkeep the land.

2. **Fertilizers** – Because plant roots extract nutrients from the soil each growing season, commercial producers and home gardeners supplement soil with fertilizers. Chemical fertilizers are added when seeding or planting, throughout the season to encourage plant growth, and at the end of the season in preparation for the following year. Over time, chemical fertilizers pollute the environment.

3. **Soil Erosion** – Heavy rains can erode soil and any nutrients associated with the soil, which can become run-off into lakes and rivers and consequently pollute the environment. The estimated annual costs of public and environmental health losses related to soil erosion exceed $45 billion each year.

4. **Money** – Soil erosion and decomposition over time can cause homeowners to buy new soil each year. Commercial farmers also spend thousands in fertilizers each year, keeping costs high.

5. **Soil Variability** – At any given time, the chemical and physical properties of soil can vary considerably from clay-like soil to sand to unproductive dirt, which can reduce vegetable production, quality and access.

6. **Absorption** – Soil absorbs the water applied to plants and vegetables. When the soil is dry, it holds onto any available water, making the water unavailable for plant roots. Soil consumes and absorbs water where sand holds and releases water.

7. **Critters** – Bugs, worms, insects and spiders inhabit the soil and can either help or hinder plant growth. Underground ant hills, animals that bore holes in the ground and random bugs crawl, creep and interface with your vegetables. Some insects even feed on vegetable plant roots and burrow deep inside to lay eggs to complete their life cycle.

8. **Topsoil** – The consumption of topsoil is a major environmental concern. Without topsoil, little plant life is possible. Conventional agriculture encourages the depletion of topsoil. Sustainable techniques attempt to slow erosion to build organic matter in the soil. The United States alone loses 2 billion tons of topsoil per year. Topsoil loss is an ecological concern as one inch of topsoil can take 500 years to form naturally.

Contemporary Gravel Applications in Gardening

Agricultural historians likely know that the agricultural community was once led and operated by geologists (Shaler, 1891). This reference to geologists as agents within the crop production community is the oldest reference found to date. During this period in the late 1800s, the definition of soil developed as "crushed or disintegrated rock and humus." This classification is still used in dictionaries today as it was defined by a geologist. By the 1930s, other scientists asserted that soil was an independent layer of earth and was to be considered independent from any rock classification (Gedroiz, 1927). From this point on, the agriculture community focused its study on soil as the primary growing medium for crops and vegetation. Attempts have been made to grow plants with land-based rocks but were determined to be ineffective (Soil Survey Division, 1993).

Contemporary scientists and researchers have touched on different forms of using rocks or gravel in agricultural production or sustainment. The University of Missouri developed the Missouri Gravel Bed, a method for using gravel to store bare root trees during the winter. In December, certain types of farmed trees are dug up and stored bare root, where the roots are exposed without any soil. These roots are semi-dormant. The application with the Missouri Gravel Bed is that the roots are better sustained if placed in gravel instead of being wrapped and held in cold storage. In the final report, they indicate that gravel, and the way they configure it, is not a growing method but a method to help sustain semi-dormant root systems (Starbuck, 2006).

One may find an essential text in the relevant work for geological agriculture in the book *Rocks for Crops* by Dr. Peter Van Straaten, who outlines the principles of *agrogeology*. Straaten is a noted faculty member of the Land Resource Science Department at the University of Guelph in Ontario, Canada. He defines agrogeology as, "the application of geology to agricultural practice, examining how soil nutrients, pH, and soil structure can be improved using naturally occurring, mineral-rich rock materials. Rocks such as potash, gypsum, limestone, and dolomite are rich in nutrients and can be used as fertilizers – directly added to the soil. One of the biggest challenges is replacing and increasing phosphates in the ground. Geologists can play a significant role in identifying, mapping and utilizing phosphate-rich rocks. Rocks such as scoria and pumice can be used to help retain water in the soil, and rocks such as limestone and dolomite can be used to decrease the acidity of the soil, raising the pH." (Straaten, 2005)

A non-profit group out of Massachusetts (www.remineralize.org) is assisting the worldwide movement of re-mineralizing soils with finely ground rock dust, sea minerals and other natural and sustainable means to increase the growth, health and nutrient value of all plant life. Adding minerals and trace elements is vital to the creation of fertile soils, healthy crops and forests, and is a key strategy to stabilize the climate. This group works in Costa Rica and other places using rock dust to act as fertilizers to soil (Campe, n.d.).

13

Contemporary Gravel Applications in Gardening

In a sense, the industry already uses rocks in agriculture with standard applications summarized below:

1) Gravel is a common mulch, but the plant's roots are extracting its nutrient from the soil underneath.

2) Gravel-filled vases of bamboo plants are attractive but the bamboo did not grow from seed in the gravel.

3) The Missouri Gravel Bed is a method of storing bare root trees in gravel during the winter, but the trees grew in the ground.

4) Hydroponics uses gravel as a growing substrate, but hydroponics is a costly indoor system that requires constant electricity and fertilized water to provide nutrients to plants and rocks when in use.

5) Agrogeology out of Canada claims that you can add select rocks to soil and use rocks as a fertilizer, but here soil is still the primary growing environment.

6) Remineralization is the process of taking rocks and crushing them to dust and adding them as a fertilizer to the ground, and here the plant is growing soil, and the rock dust is applied once.

7) Rocks are decorative stones in gardening and landscaping, but the intent here is a decoration of growing areas, not crop production.

8) Construction efforts use river rock in mixing cement, as a drainage layer and for moisture control, each void of agriculture interface.

Most of these relevant methods are similar in concept to geological agriculture. These methods substantiate the foundation that rocks may have nutrients suitable for plant life sustainment to some degree. Gravel gardening takes these processes a step further by configuring a rocks-only approach to grow crops. With previous methods, users intend for rock to fertilize the soil. With geological agriculture, rock is the growing medium instead of soil.

Geological agriculture is different in that you can cultivate crops outdoors or indoors from seed to full harvest for many years in gravel-only environments absent of fertilizer and soil. The materials required, include sedimentary gravel, sand, plastic, cotton fabric, limited water and seeds. The fertilizers and nutrients for the plants come from the gravel, and the sand is used to store the water.

Geological Agriculture Definitions

To better understand the science behind gravel gardening and the Campbell Equation, we must first explore the relevant definitions related to geology and agriculture. The next few pages provide definitions that begin with geological references and then move into agricultural and general sciences definitions.

Rocks – A relatively hard, naturally occurring mineral material. Rock can consist of a single mineral or of several minerals that are either tightly compacted or held together by a cement-like mineral matrix. The three main types of rock are igneous, sedimentary and metamorphic.

Sedimentary rocks - A type of rock that forms by the deposition of material at the Earth's surface and within bodies of water (rivers, lakes and oceans). Sedimentation is the collective name for processes that cause mineral and/or organic particles (detritus) to settle and accumulate into a rock. Particles that form a sedimentary rock by accumulating are called sediment. Before being deposited, sediment was formed by weathering and erosion in a source area, and then transported to the place of deposition by water, wind, mass movement or glaciers, which are called agents of denudation. The sedimentary rock cover of the continents of the Earth's crust is extensive. Most sedimentary rocks contain either quartz (especially siliciclastic rocks) or calcite (especially carbonate rocks). However, the origin of the minerals in a sedimentary rock is often more complex than those in an igneous rock. Minerals in a sedimentary rock have formed by precipitation during sedimentation.

Lithification - The process of converting soft, unconsolidated sediments into hard rock.

Limestone - A sedimentary rock consisting predominantly of calcium carbonate, varieties of which are formed from the skeletons of marine microorganisms and coral.

Calcite - A common constituent of sedimentary rocks, limestone in particular, much of which is formed from the shells of dead marine organisms. Approximately 10% of sedimentary rock is limestone.

Sand - A sedimentary material consisting of small, often rounded grains or particles of disintegrated rock, smaller than granules and larger than silt. Although sand often consists of quartz, it can consist of any other mineral or rock fragment as well. Coral sand, for example, consists of limestone fragments. Sand is used as drainage properties in construction and other industries.

Geological Agriculture Definitions

Now it is time to review key definitions of gardening and agriculture.

Soil – The portion of the Earth's surface consisting of disintegrated rock and humus.

Germination – The beginning of growth, as of a seed, spore or bud. The germination of most seeds and spores occurs in response to warmth and water. Dormant seeds are very dry and require the absorption of water to initiate the metabolic processes of respiration and begin to digest their stored food. Respiration requires the presence of oxygen, which must be sufficiently available in the soil for germination to proceed, so the soil must be wet but not so waterlogged as to make oxygen inaccessible. Temperatures must be above freezing (zero degrees Celsius) but not excessively hot (not more than about 45 degrees Celsius). If conditions are right, a radicle (an embryonic root) emerges from the seed coat, anchoring the seed; it then grows and puts out lateral roots.

Nitrogen fixation – The process by which free nitrogen from the air is combined with other elements to form inorganic compounds, such as ammonium ions, which can then be converted by nitrification into nutrients that can be readily absorbed by plants and other organisms for incorporation into more complex organic compounds. Atmospheric nitrogen is also fixed industrially under high pressure and heat to form ammonia, as in the production of fertilizers. All living organisms are dependent on nitrogen fixation and would ultimately die without it.

Nitrogen cycle – The continuous sequence of events by which atmospheric nitrogen and nitrogenous compounds in the soil are converted, as by nitrification and nitrogen fixation, into substances that can be utilized by green plants, with the substances returning to the air and soil as a result of the decay of the plants and denitrification.

Plants – Structure, growth and development - Most of the solid material in a plant is taken from the atmosphere. Through a process known as photosynthesis, most plants use the energy in sunlight to convert carbon dioxide from the atmosphere, plus water, into simple sugars. (Parasitic plants, on the other hand, use the resources of its host to grow.) These sugars are then used as building blocks and form the main structural component of the plant. Chlorophyll, a green-colored, magnesium-containing pigment is essential to this process; it is generally present in plant leaves, and often in other plant parts as well.

More Key Definitions from Agriculture

Plants – Plants usually rely on soil primarily for support and water (in quantitative terms), but also obtain compounds of nitrogen, phosphorus, potassium, magnesium and other elemental nutrients. Epiphytic and lithophytic plants depend on air and nearby debris for nutrients, and carnivorous plants supplement their nutrient requirements with insect prey that they capture. For the majority of plants to grow successfully they also require oxygen in the atmosphere and around their roots (soil gas) for respiration. Plants use oxygen and glucose (which may be produced from stored starch) to provide energy. Some plants grow as submerged aquatics, using oxygen dissolved in the surrounding water, and a few specialized vascular plants, such as mangroves, can grow with their roots in anoxic conditions.

Phosphorus – The vast majority of phosphorus compounds are consumed as fertilizers. Phosphate minerals are fossils. Low phosphate levels are an important limit to growth in some aquatic systems. The chief commercial use of phosphorus compounds for production of fertilizers is due to the need to replace the phosphorus that plants remove from the soil, and its annual demand is rising nearly twice as fast as the growth of the human population.

The phosphorus cycle originates in sediments, the main reservoir for phosphates, while rainwater contains a minimal amount of this nutrient, so it is classified as a sedimentary cycle. However, substantial environmental damage is a product of mining phosphorous deposits on islands. The major source of phosphorus in soil is apatite, a calcium-phosphate mineral, and the weathering of terrestrial deposits releases phosphorus, some of which goes into rivers, lakes, or oceans. Plants absorb phosphorus in the form of phosphate, and herbivores consume the plants, taking in the nutrient. Phosphate is then released back to the soil or water source by animal excretion; this recycling process is a significant source of phosphorous in freshwater ecosystems. Also, when organisms die, the decomposers reduce the phosphorus into organic forms, returning it to the soil, which aids the cycle in continuing.

Geological Agriculture Definitions

Hydrology – The scientific study of the properties, distribution and effects of water on the Earth's surface, in the soil and underlying rocks, and in the atmosphere.

Water – A clear, colorless, tasteless, odorless liquid that is essential for plant and animal life and constitutes, in impure form, rain, oceans, rivers, lakes, etc. It is a neutral substance, an effective solvent for many compounds, and is used as a standard for many physical properties.

Leaching – To leach or leaching is the process by which components, particles or aspects of a substance emit off part of itself into a new environment. Leaching is similar to dissolving, but the substance does not dissolve, but rather erodes small microscopic layers of itself into another environment. With gravel, nutrients leach out of the rocks and settle in the available water for plant use.

Condensation – The change of the physical state of matter from gaseous phase into liquid phase. Condensation commonly occurs when a vapor is cooled and/or compressed to its saturation limit when the molecular density in the gas phase reaches its maximal threshold. Water is the product of its vapor condensation. Psychrometry measures the rates of condensation from and evaporation into the air moisture at various atmospheric pressures and temperatures. Many substances are hygroscopic, meaning they attract water, usually in proportion to the relative humidity or above a critical relative humidity. Such substances include cotton, paper, cellulose, other wood products, sugar, calcium oxide or limestone.

Definition Sources adapted and sourced from :

https://www.merriam-webster.com
www.dictionary.com
www.Wikipedia.com
http://geology.com

Gravel Gardening Basics

The most important definitions are those related to sedimentary rocks. The sediment in the word sedimentary relates to organic materials such as dead fish, decayed leaves, wood chips and other sediment that exists in water or is washed out to sea. Much of the sediment that creates sedimentary rocks were once organic life of some sort.

A foundational reality of sedimentary rock is that it leaches or disperses organic materials or nutrients when impacted with water. This rock type, which is largely limestone-based, is also a key element in the living coral reef. In the ocean waters, the reef provides life to thousands of species. The same principal appears to apply on land. When sedimentary rock impacts water, a chemical action occurs where the molecules of the water attach with the molecules of the rocks to create nutrient-enriched water on the surface of the gravel. The gravel itself also acts as a support system and structure for plant growth. Water enables these "organic" rocks to leach out nutrients capable of supporting root systems for plants and vegetation. Since the origin of the nutrients is a rock material, the rock should leach nutrients for many years.

The rest of the gravel garden configuration is designed to maintain consistent moisture within the sedimentary rocks to create a sustainable root development ecosystem. The primary ingredient to control for consistent moisture is the presence of sand under the gravel. Sand holds and drains water, where soil consumes or absorbs water. In a gravel garden, sand is used as a water storage area beneath the gravel to maintain a sustained moist environment enough to consistently activate the chemical action between the rocks and water. The chemical action releases nutrients from the rocks and along with water, air and temperature initiates germination of the seed. The submerged sand allows water to be stored and kept cool so that water does not evaporate due to the sun, but rather kept available to provide consistent moisture for roots.

Outdoors, we add lawn fabric to the configuration as a layer separating the gravel from the underlying soil. The fabric not only creates a semi-enclosed environment, but it spreads water evenly from beneath the gravel. The fabric also prevents weed growth since it is layered between the gravel and soil preventing underground weeds from growing. When configured properly, the capillary properties within the sand, fabric and gravel allow the gravel bed to evenly disperse moisture. The moisture enables the chemical action to take place and provide consistent nutrients to root systems. When watered appropriately, the moist environment sustains plants. As water, nutrients and natural air provide growth support for seeds and roots systems within the gravel beneath the surface, nitrogen fixation and sunlight provide the rest of the ingredients for plant growth and a sustained all-natural growing ecosystem on top of the soil.

Water Testing

The water testing chart below depicts the water test results for the type of gravel used to grow most of the plants in this book. Tap water and tap water that has settled in gravel for 10 days were compared and tested. Test results revealed several differences between regular tap water and the tap water steeped in gravel. The results uncovered that gravel removes certain contaminants such as iron, manganese, zinc and inorganic nitrates, making the water cleaner.

These contaminants were detected at or above the minimum detection level, but not above the EPA standards.					
All numbers is noted in milligrams per liter					
Contaminant	**Regular Tap Water**	**Gravel Sample**	**Difference**	**% Difference**	**Effect**
MICROBIOLOGICALS					
Coliform	Absent	Present*	0	Not present in tap water	Added
INORGANIC ANALYTES - METALS					
Calcium	48.1	48.5	0.4	1%	Increased
Copper	0.009	0.011	0.002	18%	Increased
Iron	0.025	0	-0.025	Not present in gravel	Removed
Magnesium	11	9.7	-1.3	-13%	Lowered
Manganese	0.005	0	-0.005	Not present in gravel	Removed
Potassium	3.6	4.7	1.1	23%	Increased
Silica	5.42	7.61	2.19	29%	Increased
Sodium	27	27	0	0%	Same
Zinc	0.015	0.004	-0.011	-275%	Lowered
PHYSICAL FACTORS					
Alkalinity	92	90	-2	-2%	Lowered
Hardness	170	160	-10	-6%	Lowered
PH	7.2	7.9	0.7	9%	Increased
Total Dissolved Solids	280	260	-20	-8%	Lowered
Turbidity	0.2	1	0.8	80%	Increased
INORGANIC ANALYTES					
Chloride	43	39	-4	-10%	Lowered
Fluoride	1.7	0.8	-0.9	-113%	Lowered
Nitrate as N	1.4	0	-1.4	Not present in gravel	Removed
Sulfate	86	69	-17	-25%	Lowered
ORGANIC ANALYTES - TRIHALOMETHANES					
Bromodichloromethane	0.004	0	-0.004	Not present in gravel	Removed
Chloroform	0.015	0	-0.015	Not present in gravel	Removed
Total THMs	0.019	0	-0.019	Not present in gravel	Removed
ORGANIC ANALYTES - VOLATILES					
Acetone	0	0.01	0.01	Not present in tap water	Added
*Above the standard, but not an enforeceable EPA action.					

Conversely, there is an increase in potassium, copper, silica, coliform and turbidity. These items represent the additional elements added to the water for root sustainment. Potassium, up 23% after 10 days, is the second most important nutrient needed for plant growth after nitrogen, which already is present due to nitrogen fixation. Potassium is a key nutrient for the plant's tolerance to stresses such as cold and heat, drought, wear and pest problems. Copper, up 18%, is an essential nutrient for plant growth and because only a small amount is needed, it is classified as a micro-nutrient. Copper is an important component of proteins found in the enzymes that regulate the rate of many biochemical reactions in plants.

Plants would not grow without the presence of these specific enzymes. Research projects show that copper: 1) promotes seed production and formation; 2) plays an essential role in chlorophyll formation; and 3) is essential for proper enzyme activity. The silica, up 29%, on the other hand, is not as helpful to plants and it is theorized that this feature may alter the effects of growth, causing the need to test gravel types of the crops you seek to grow before adopting these methods more comprehensively in a given household or business.

The effects of the added presence of coliform is expected given the sedimentary composition of the rocks. And finally, the 80% increase in turbidity, which is the cloudiness or haziness of a fluid caused by individual particles (suspended solids) that are generally invisible to the naked eye, indicates the addition of new compounds into the water. The measurement of turbidity is a key test of water quality and substantiates that the rocks are emitting materials into the water.

The initial basic water test represents the tip of the iceberg of capability and capacity of river rock as a component of agriculture, plant health and ultimately human health, which are all are interrelated. The test identified that the gravel acts as a sponge for certain contaminants while leaching out nutrients at the same time. The dual benefits of gravel enables it to both clean and feed the water that impacts the gravel. The new gravel water is now available to feed root systems.

Further tests will need to be conducted to identify and specify the exact molecular transfer in and out of the gravel and to what degree. Given that most river rock is a collection of 5 to 12 different types of rock mixed together, some rocks will absorb containments and leach nutrients at a different rate with varying concentrations of elements leaching out in various amounts.

The dual clean and feed nature of gravel is only a part of the characteristics of gravel. Additional observations reveal that gravel sweats naturally in heat, creating moisture. The presence of moisture activates the process, enabling gravel to create its water and start the germination process for certain seed types under high heat. The tests and observations suggests that gravel has three key inherent characteristic in high temperatures: 1) creates moisture; 2) cleans moisture; and 3) improves the moisture. It will take years for society to know which of the thousands of types of rocks is the most effective at producing crops.

In 2015 some began to ask what effects gravel water might have on other organic life beyond plants. Given the fundamentals of the Campbell Equation, it is possible that Water + River Rock = More than plant food. Studies in 2018 and beyond will look at ancillary effects of gravel water in other environments.

Nutrition Testing

Cucumbers grown in gravel in 2010 were tested in a nutrition laboratory and found to be near identical to the USDA standards for a cucumber. The nutrients facts below on the left are from the cucumbers grown in the gravel garden. As shown, these cucumbers are good sources of vitamin A and vitamin C with no sodium and low in sugars. The normal cucumber nutrition facts are depicted on the right next to the colored maps. Notice that the gravel-grown cucumbers appear to be more nutritious with more fiber, vitamin A and C, and calcium. There also appears to be more carbohydrates , dietary fiber, and sugar in the gravel grown cucumbers.

Cucumbers grown in gravel Nutrition Facts

Nutrition Facts

Serving Size (100g)
Servings Per Container

Amount Per Serving

Calories 15	Calories from Fat 0

	% Daily Value*
Total Fat 0g	0%
Saturated Fat 0g	0%
Trans Fat 0g	
Cholesterol 0mg	0%
Sodium 0mg	0%
Total Carbohydrate 4g	1%
Dietary Fiber 1g	4%
Sugars 2g	
Protein 1g	

Vitamin A 2%	•	Vitamin C 4%
Calcium 2%	•	Iron 2%

*Percent Daily Values are based on a 2,000 calorie diet. Your daily values may be higher or lower depending on your calorie needs:

	Calories	2,000	2,500
Total Fat	Less Than	65g	80g
Saturated Fat	Less Than	20g	25g
Cholesterol	Less Than	300mg	300 mg
Sodium	Less Than	2,400mg	2,400mg
Total Carbohydrate		300g	375g
Dietary Fiber		25g	30g

Calories per gram:
Fat 9 • Carbohydrate 4 • Protein 4

Cucumbers grown in soil Nutrition Facts.

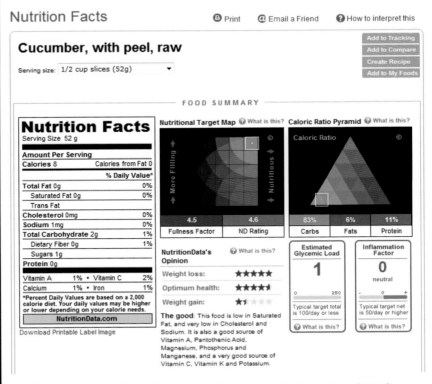

http://nutritiondata.self.com/facts/vegetables-and-vegetable-products/2439/2

Chapter 1 Summary

The fundamentals of geological agriculture shared in Chapter 1 lays out the foundation of the science, drawing on and merging known definitions to derive the components of this unknown science. The key takeaways below provide the building blocks for the science for effective indoor and outdoor applications.

Sedimentary rock – Sedimentary rock leaches nutrient material when wet, capable of supporting plant life. Geologists have not historically studied sedimentary rock for its nutrient value relative to supporting plant life. Sedimentary rock differs in geologic formation in each of the rivers, lakes and oceans of the world, suggesting that each rock around the world formed in water may leach nutrient matter when impacted with water.

The water test - The water test identified the exact nutrient compounds sedimentary rock leaches to support plant life. The stark increase in potassium, silica and copper in water steeped in sedimentary rock provides the nutrient mix to support an ongoing growing ecosystem for plants. This test also provides a roadmap for how to study, test and monitor what is being added to the growing environment.

Benefits, benefits, benefits – The stated benefits of geological agriculture are significant given the lack of man-made materials used for ongoing long-term plant production. The option of producing food permanently from rock provides humanity with the benefit of taking one step closer to achieving global food security where all have access to nutrition regardless of the availability of soils, fertilizers, electricity and other man-made products.

Configuration – With the basic Campbell Equation of Sedimentary Rock + Water = Nutrient Materials (plant food), the rest of the process is configuration. The key to geological agriculture is configuring the sedimentary rock in a manner that keeps it moist and supportive of root structures that can feed on moist rock.

How science missed this – When land-based rocks failed the test to show that they can support plant life, science did not think to give water-based rocks a chance. Moreover, few academic institutions possess both a geology department and an agriculture department necessary for the academic community to have discovered the possibility and refine it. This chapter ultimately helped explain how and why modern science seemingly missed this apparently simple process of crop production.

Ag industry apathy – Given the lack of knowledge on the subject, agricultural professionals tend to doubt geological agriculture due to the historic myth that rocks are inert not capable of supporting life. This book tells a different tale but so far big agriculture is slow to acknowledge the possibility, electing to not investigate, research nor refine the process.

With the basic elements of geological agriculture shared in Chapter 1, Chapter 2 discusses indoor applications of the science while Chapter 3 looks at outdoor applications.

Chapter 2
Indoor Gravel
Gardening

Test First

Before you convert large areas of land into gravel gardens, test a variety of locally available gravel and seed types that you seek to grow. Once you purchase a variety of river pea gravel bags from available stores, you can test the gravel's effectiveness by using the gravel, sand and an empty clear plastic cup or recycled water bottle.

Simply puncture tiny holes in the bottom of the plastic cup for drainage and along the sides for air. Fill ¼ of the cup with sand and then gravel. Pour small seeds on top to fall through the cracks between the gravel. Place large seeds in the center of the gravel. Water to the top and let the water drip into a drip tray. Refill the water when the drip tray is dry.

Wheatgrass in Miami Beach rock

The images on this page show five different sedimentary or river rock tests from Miami Beach rock; Outer Banks, NC, beach rocks; Ace Hardware store-bought rock; Tennessee river rock and rocks from Chesapeake Bay, MD. Plants grew from seed in each case, testing both quick growing edibles and common crops.

As you can see, the fundamentals are the same, sand on the bottom and gravel on the top. Once you set up your cup tests and drop in a few seeds, it should take about 10 days to determine if the gravel will work with the seeds you are trying to grow. If they do, then feel free to set up outdoor gravel gardens. You should, however, only convert a small percentage of your space in the first year to determine the full cycle of the crop you are trying to grow. Refer to Chapter 3 for outdoor gardens.

Micro greens in Outer Banks, NC beach rocks.

Some plants can mature in the small cup while others will need to be transplanted. If you choose to do this, it is best to transplant to soil versus into another gravel environment. Roots tend to be fragile where rocks tend to be hard. Transplant shock is likely from rock to rock.

Beans, peas and squash in Ace Hardware rock

Micro Greens and Peas in Chesapeake Bay rock.

Arugula in Tennessee river rock.

The basics steps for configuring an indoor gravel grow cup is as follows:

1.   Puncture tiny holes in the plastic cup using a safety pin, needle or bobby pin. Puncture six holes at the bottom spaced evenly apart for drainage and four holes halfway on the cup spaced evenly apart for air.

2.   Fill ¼ of the cup with sand. Puncture four tiny holes in the cup where the sand is located on the sides and bottom. This will allow the sand to breath from the sides.

3.   Next, fill gravel halfway to the top and then place your seed in the cup. Fill the cup with gravel.

4.   Pour small tiny seeds on top to fall through the cracks. Shake the cup so that the seeds fall through the cracks so that they are half way in the gravel. Seeds will not germinate in sand.

5.   Place large seeds in the center of the gravel. You can pour the gravel half way, put in seeds and then pour in the gravel to the top.

6.   Place the gravel grow cup on a drip tray.

7.   Water to the top and let the water drip into a drip tray.

8.   Refill water when the drip tray is dry, which is usually after 4 to 10 days depending on room evaporation rates.

9.   Once a crop has grown to full term, you can harvest, empty out the gravel and roots and start over from step 2 or 3.

There are three primary layers to the gravel growing ecosystem: Top or dry layer; Middle or moist or active layer; and the Bottom or wet or sand layer. The top layer is always dry and serves to help insulate moisture below. The active middle layer is where the growth process is occurring where the rock is wet and feeding the roots. The bottom sand layer serves as irrigation control drawing in water as necessary from the drip tray. Image shown was taken out of the drip tray.

Large bean seed

Dry layer

Moist layer

Wet layer

Puncture 4 tiny holes where the sand is on the sides and bottom of the cup. Puncture 4 holes on opposite sides of the moist layer. Use a tack or safety pin to puncture the holes.

The images below depict the steps of assembling your gravel grow cup. The key step is to puncture the bottom and sides of the plastic cup with tiny holes with a tack or nail as shown in photos 2 and 3 below. Puncture holes at the bottom and on the sides. Image 4 shows a tiny hole where the sand is located. The holes will provide oxygen into the gravel grow cup. Image 7 shows a cup of water next to the gravel grow cup. Image 8 illustrates that by pouring ½ cup of water in the grow cup, the water will rise to the top and then drain into the drip tray.

Cups with properly placed sand, seeds and gravel tend to germinate where roots grow towards the sand while the shoots grow towards the surface. The moisture layer is constantly feeding the heart of the plant nutrients from the gravel. Photo 2 shows bean mix sprouts after two days and photo 3 depicts the beans after seven days. In photo 4, the sunflower sprouts after two days while photo 5 was taken after seven days. Some plants will grow faster than others. For the micro greens and sprouts, these plants are ready to harvest at 2-3 inches and serve as nutritious snacks.

1

2 – Bean Mix at 2 days

3 – Bean Mix at 7 days

4 – Sunflower sprouts at 2 days

5 – Sunflower sprouts 7 days

Micro greens and sprouts are ideal for gravel grow cups as they allow fresh nutrition in a short period of time. One pack of seeds can produce gravel grow snacks for many months.

Gravel Grow Cup – Handling

1. Place cup on drip tray

    a.   Plastic drip trays are ideal as terracotta drip trays and ceramic pots absorb water out of the drip tray.

2. Water

    a.   Water the cup to the top of the cup. You should only need ½ cups of water.

    b.   Water will drain into the drip tray as a result of the tiny holes. Allow the water to drain and do not add any more until the drip tray is dry.

    c.   Water from the top when the drip tray is empty.

    d.   Depending on the temperature, ½ cup of water can last a day or a week. The higher the indoor temperature, the more you will need to water as evaporation will occur. If you keep the environment at 70 degrees indoors, then ½ cup a water can last a week. Once plants are growing well they will consumer more water, so anticipate watering once a week.

3. Observe

    a.   Being a clear cup, you will notice in a few days the seeds on the side begin to open and germinate, letting out the roots and shoots.

    b.   Every day you will notice growth and after about 14 to 20 days you can harvest and snack on the healthy micro greens and sprouts if that is what was planted.

    c.   Common garden crops will also grow and emerge after 14 to 20 days, but can need to be transplanted to soil. Common crops will crowd out in the cups and can need transplanting. Some legumes can go to full term in gravel but they will not be as robust as outdoors given the sunlight.

4. Repeat

    a.   Once you have eaten all that the gravel grow cup has to offer or after you transplant the crops, you can pour out the gravel and sand onto a plate and start over.

    b.   Remove loose roots and seeds.

    c.   Wash out the cup with soap and water and dry.

    d.   Put sand back into the cup first to ½ inch.

    e.   Put gravel back into the cup.

    f.   Try other seeds in the cup. To Soil Less recommends Botanical Interests seeds for micro greens and sprout edibles. Peas and beans seeds are also recommended. Most types of crops will not grow to full term in a gravel grow cup. Only edibles and certain types of legumes will mature in a gravel grow cup. Other seedlings will need to be transplanted to soil.

    g.   Place seeds in the center of the gravel.

    h.   Place the cup back on the drip tray and start the watering process.

    i.   You will be able to continue growing in this cup for years to come.

Gravel Grow Cups In Action – Seven Days Later

During the height of winter we wanted to test a variety of crop types in gravel grow cups or similar recycled growing environments. We took old plastic containers of lemonade, cranberry and other soda bottles to configure them as recycled growing environments. The photos below of 11 items depict growth after seven days from seed. Only ½ cup of water was used in most cases except where the recycled growing space is larger. As you will see, the geological growing environment seems suitable for a variety of plant types and offers the notion of indoor winter gardening as an alternative source for nutrition indoors in a relative short period of time.

String Beans

Lima Beans

Alfalfa Sprouts

Bean Sprouts

Marigolds

Peas

Scallions

Sunflower

Pea Shoots

Corn

Lettuce

Fourteen days later, 15 plants have well-developed structures. The pea shoots micro greens and bean sprouts have fully matured, requiring harvesting. Common crops, however, are just getting started. Some will mature in the cups but transplanting and thinning will be needed for other plants.

String Beans

Lima Beans

Squash

Bean Sprouts

Spinach

Iris

Peas

Scallions

Cucumbers

Sunflower

Pea Shoots

Corn

Lettuce

Cosmos

Marigolds

Many plants will grow at an inch per day in a gravel grow cup, requiring a trellis to help support the growing plants. A roll of chicken coop wire was purchased and cut into small trellis ladders as shown below with pea shoots, squash and beans. These plants tend to need a trellis after 8 to 10 days. Other household items can be used as a gravel grow cup trellis including a wire hanger that is straighten out and then bent in a U shape with each end going into the cup. A stick, pole and a pencil can help a plant stay upright in a gravel grow cup.

Squash

Pea Shoots

Beans

Gravel Grow Cup – Handling - Seeding

How many seeds to plant in a gravel grow cup is a common question. However, since the upper limits of the gravel nutrient output is unknown, seeding liberally is suitable. With the plants below, beans, peas, squash and okra will have 7 to 15 seeds planted. With pea shoots 10 to 20 seeds can be planted while cilantro, lettuce and wheatgrass can have 20 to 40 seeds planted in the gravel grow cup. Conversely, due to size, only 1 hyacinth bulb can be planted in a gravel grow cup. The gravel grow cup is an active ecosystem constantly producing nutrients, making the system capable of supporting many seeds within a small space.

Roots grow shorter and wrap around the rocks and layer themselves for space efficiency. Eventually, for many plants the ecosystem will begin to overload and decay and will need to start over.

Cilantro

Pea Shoots

Hyacinth

Squash

Wheatgrass

Okra

Beans

Peas

Lettuce

An indoor gravel growing location can quickly turn into an indoor micro-farm. As plants grow, watering frequency will increase. The growing plant roots will require more water to sustain the growth. Some plants will consume water at a faster rate than others. Shown below are a variety of seed types planted at the same time with the images taken after three weeks. The beans and pea shoots tend to grow the fastest. When planning an indoor gravel gardening area, expect to eventually attract bugs, so it is helpful to have a bug light onsite. With the growing ecosystems of various plants, the new plant life will also create new bacteria and nates. Plants that you can eat right away like cilantro, pea shoots, wheatgrass and other micro greens, sprouts and spices can do well indoors. Bean and pea plants will go to full term, but the squash, tomatoes, cucumbers, okra and other stemmed plants will need to be transplanted.

A central aspect of the gravel grow cup is to test what grows indoors and develop an outdoor version to grow the plant better. All plants tend to perform better in outdoor gravel gardens than in an indoor gravel grow cup. Outdoor organics (bees, bugs, sun, etc.) tend to have a positive effect on the plant outcome. The next few pages discuss specific plant types and how they evolve and grow in a gravel grow cup.

Basil does OK in gravel. These images are of a basil plant that is about two months old. Basil grows slow and low in gravel unlike in soil, where basil can grow much higher and faster. Plants like basil growing in gravel can be referred to as micro-basil. Although small in comparison, the gravel-grown basil does carry a strong taste. Further testing is suggested using a variety of basil seed types to determine which will grow best. Having a dozen of these growing will provide organic spice to life.

Cilantro grows well in the gravel grow cup indoors. After about three weeks, the height of the cilantro is as shown. Lee Williams grew his cilantro on a windowsill in Los Angeles (top left). After the third week he was able to harvest a little bit each day, enjoying daily fresh cilantro for four weeks. Cilantro tends to grow better in the gravel grow cup indoors than in outdoor gravel gardens. The temperature-controlled indoor environment is more ideal for cilantro, making this a suitable spice for the windowsill gardener.

Gravel Grow Cups In Action – Lettuce

Feb 15

Feb 23

Mar 5

Mar 23

Lettuce grows in gravel into an edible and delicious micro lettuce bush-like plant nothing like how lettuce grows full term in an outdoor environment. The gravel grow cup version of lettuce matures after about 6 to 7 weeks. The lettuce here was planted on Feb 1 and by March 23 had grown to all it was going to do before crowding out the root system and killing the plant. From a taste perspective, harvesting anytime after four weeks is possible as this crop is edible at any time by simply cutting above the rocks, adding some salad dressing and enjoying micro lettuce as a nutritious snack.

A key observation with lettuce is the number of seeds that germinate and grow. The March 5 photo depicts the roots in what is likely 50 to 100 lettuce seeds all growing in this 9-ounce space. The roots do not appear as crowded as other root structures and the lettuce grew another month after that photo was taken.

The plant type is ideal for those seeking micro lettuce salads on an ongoing basis. This lettuce is also tasty without salad dressing. At trade shows guests snack on the lettuce while at the booth, citing its fresh flavor.

Gravel Grow Cups In Action – String Beans

Beans are likely the most reliable seed type of common crops to grow to full term, as they will mature into a bean within 6 to 7 weeks in the gravel grow cup. The bean plant on the far left was grown under six CLF lights held 6 inches above the plant, adjusting the lights up periodically as the plant grew. This plant grew 20 inches in 22 days from seed. As shown, the leaf span is broad and horizontal. This plant was just entering into its flowering phase when the photo was taken. The bean plant in the center and to the right was six weeks old when the photo was taken depicting harvestable string bean both in the foreground of the photo on the right and in the background in the same photo in the upper left-hand corner. The plant in the center portrays a less full leaf span and leaves that are sagging even though beans grew to a harvestable state. The key takeaway is that light matters. The image on the left had ideal light 6 inches from the plant, while the image on the right and center had normal house lights 3 to 6 feet from the plant. The 22-day old plant is more robust than the six-week old plant. By comparing the three-week against the six-week bean plants, the effects of light is stark and encourages homeowners and growers to set up their growing area so that lights have height adjustment and can be 6 inches away from the top of the plant, raising up as the plant grows.

Another common aspect to string beans growing in the gravel grow cup is that they will always need a trellis to remain upright. The height of the trellis should be 18 to 24 inches and it will aid in the growth and development of the plant. Bean seeds can grow up to an inch per day or more depending on the light source. Bean seeds are also the primary test seed of the science when testing new rock types due to their reliability and global food demand for beans.

3 weeks

6 weeks

6 weeks

Peas will grow to full term in the gravel grow cup after about 7 to 8 weeks. The pea plant will undergo a nice flower phase with white pea blossoms in advance of the actual pea pod. Like all plants, light matters, but these peas grew under normal indoor CFL lights. Although a strong light would aid in its development, peas will grow to full term with or without strong light. Peas require a trellis which should be 10 to 16 inches high to accommodate the anticipated growth.

Peas, like beans, are one of the few common crop types that grow to full term in the gravel grow cup. Consequently, pea seeds are also used as a test seed. Both peas and beans are consumed worldwide, making the gravel grow cup an ideal method for growing these plant types seemingly anywhere sedimentary rock is found. A person who staggers the planting of 60 gravel grow cups over 60 days will harvest the first set of peas in cup one on the 60th day and the next cup of peas the next day and so forth. As long as the person keeps re-planting at each harvest they will have a permanent source of peas. One $6 bag of pea gravel can make 65 gravel grow cups.

Gravel Grow Cups In Action – Asiatic Lily

The Asiatic lily bulb test revealed that Asiatic lilies can grow in gravel, but the outcome is hit or miss. Three bulbs were planted but only one grew to full bloom with vibrant colors. The bulb matured after four months. All bulbs were placed in 16-ounce gravel grow cups; the space appeared to be enough for this complex plant, but it is unknown why the remaining two plants didn't make it.

The seed quality could be a factor as well as physical handling when moving plants around, which could damage roots. There are about 6 to 12 different rock types in a gravel grow cup. In theory, one rock type is likely leaching more of a specific nutrient than another. In this case, the placement of the bulb on a random set of rocks may lead to why one bulb grows better than another. Bulb A may happen to have the heart of the bulb touching a specific rock that leaches a specific nutrient. Theoretically, the heart of bulb B may be placed on another rock that leaches less of the specific nutrient, causing bulb B to perform and grow less than bulb A.

1 month

2 months

4th month

2 months

4th month

The begonia bulb placed in the 16-ounce gravel grow cup survived for about six months before it began to die out. Gravel is scalable so having a larger cup will provide more room for bigger bulbs like the begonia bulb to grow a strong root system.

Typical begonias do not grow in this fashion and this bulb type was only tested indoors. The plants as shown can be attractive for the windowsill for about 4 to 6 months. This plant is an ideal plant to transplant into a soil environment. Transplanting to a rock environment will likely damage the roots. The velvet-like texture of the leaf was an added bonus in witnessing this weird growth in gravel.

Additional testing is required with the begonia plant outdoors to determine its growth pattern and resiliency. Outdoor organics such as bees, the sun and worms play a role in plant development and would likely benefit the begonia plant.

Gravel Grow Cups In Action – Calla Lily

The calla lily bulb appears to do well in the indoor temperature-controlled environment. Also in a 16-ounce cup, this bulb was planted on March 3 and by May 5 had bloomed into the vibrant yellow calla lily plant below. The second flower grew by May 25 and by June 10 the plant died. Only one calla lily bulb was planted and it seemed to take well in the gravel growing ecosystem. The stalk of the plant was very strong and hearty enough to keep the plant upright and sturdy despite its height. The bigger cup provided the adequate space and support system.

Gravel Grow Cups In Action – Hyacinth

A 9-ounce gravel grow cup served as the growing environment for hyacinth bulbs. Each grew fragrant micro hyacinth plants. The six-week growth period provided fragrant flowers for 2 to 3 weeks. After the initial bloom died out, additional smaller flowers emerged lasting three additional weeks.

The smaller gravel grow cup contained enough space to produce the images shown. It is likely that the 16-ounce cup would yield a taller, stronger, longer-lasting plant. Hyacinth typically grow more robust than shown with one flowering cycle during the spring. The reaction to the gravel grow cup test suggests that this plant may be available to grow indoors year round, not just in the spring. Planting bulbs monthly can provide ongoing hyacinth during the fall and winter, providing natural fragrances of spring anytime indoors.

The tulip bulb in the gravel grow cup tends to grow a hybrid tulip with a poor flower. Outdoors the tulip bulbs grow better than indoors. In the 9-ounce gravel grow cup the growth cycle skipped the tulip leaf phase and went straight to the flower pod phase, growing the simple flower-only structure shown below. The lack of space may have been a factor. Tulips tend grow properly in outdoor gravel gardens (see Chapter 3).

Gravel Grow Cups In Action – Jade

During a live streaming video presentation in 2015 with blogger Brenda Haas, a guest asked about gravel and house plants. With that in mind, a store-bought jade plant was placed in a gravel grow cup. When planted on May 25 the jade plant had four leaf levels. By August 9 there were six leaf levels and by Sept 12, eight leaf levels. On January 2, the jade plant was placed near a window that was left open on a nice January day. On Jan 10, the temperature dropped to 29 degrees and the jade plant died as the window was not closed. The cold air froze the roots. Despite the cold snap, jade the houseplant seems to like gravel.

May 25, 2016

Aug 9, 2016

Sept 12, 2016

Jan 2, 2017

Jan 10, 2017

Gravel Grow Cups In Action – Aloe

The aloe plant test is likely one of the most perplexing when it comes to growing plants in gravel. The store-bought aloe plant, placed in gravel on January 15 with five visible limbs, grew to nine visible limbs by April 22. Although robust growth is apparent, an unfortunate side effect of aloe growing in gravel is that the gravel ecosystem also kills the aloe plant limbs. As more aloe limbs grow, the base limbs also tend to decay at the base and fall off of the plant. A lost or fallen aloe limb is shown below on May 5. Notice the base of the limbs on the July 25 photo on the right below where base limb decay is evident even though the plant limbs are visibly longer as shown on the July 25 photo on the left. During the growing cycle, gravel grew the number of limbs from 5 to 10 after three months but lost most of them three months later back to seven remaining limbs by late July which are much longer but seemingly destined to die.

Jan 15

Apr 22

May 5

The aloe houseplant test introduces a new aspect to growing in gravel where the gravel both helps and hurts the plant. Further testing is required.

July 25

July 25

Aug 30

By August 30, the number of aloe limbs had reduced to six with signs of growth and decay ongoing. The cup ecosystem is also beginning to decay. The plant has survived and grown for over eight months but it is likely that by the end of the year all of the limbs may fall. The limbs are much longer than they were at the onset and the weight of the limb may be contributing to the base decay process.

Aug 30

The aloe plant test suggests at first glance that one should not plant aloe in gravel. Should methods to compensate for base decay present themselves, then it is possible to derive a positive conclusion on whether to plant aloe in gravel. It is possible that a pot with a higher rim could support the limbs from falling off. Also should it be found that the aloe nutrient value is higher than soil-grown aloe, one may decide to continue to grow aloe in gravel. So far, soil-grown aloe performs better than gravel-grown aloe.

Aug 30

This book was published before the aloe test concluded.

Recycled Gravel Growing

Gravel gardens perform better in plastic containers versus contemporary pots and vases. Plastic is easier to retrofit with the tiny drainage and air holes required for effectiveness. Recycled plastic containers of lemonade, cranberry and soda bottles served as the growing environments. The photos below portray wheatgrass, marigolds and iris bulbs in recycled gallon gravel gardens. To assemble, cut the plastic bottle leaving growing space. Puncture the bottom of the plastic bottles with a knife or tac to poke small incisions into the plastic for drainage and air.

Wheatgrass, Marigolds and Iris Bulbs

Wheatgrass and Sunflower Sprouts

Pour a half-inch of sand at the bottom as shown in the red gallon image to the left. Then add about one inch of gravel, seed the area and add one more inch of gravel. Place in a bin to serve as the drip tray and water. As shown, plants tend to do well in these scaled up containers, demonstrating the scale effects of geo-ag. Scale is natural with gravel and can provide bulk nutrition like with the amount of pea shoots growing below.

Marigolds

Alfalfa Sprouts

Pea Shoots

Recycled Gravel Growing

Dr. Edwin Nichols of Washington, DC, tried his hand at taking a water bottle, cutting off the top and puncturing tiny holes at the bottom and along the sides for air. He added water and put it on the kitchen table. About 12 string bean plants are growing in the recycled gravel garden. Five weeks later the flowering phase set the stage for the coming beans. Three bean types planted in this garden should yield three bean types. Notice the leaf pattern on Aug 25, opening and spreading wide as they are facing the sun from that direction for about six hours a day. This plant demonstrates the difference between a good indoor sunlight environment and a basement environment as shown in the

prior pages. With balanced room temperature and good direct sunlight and water, many plants can do well. On Sept 10, yellow, green and purple bean types are visible. Notice the layered nature of the cup ecosystem; dry on top, wet at the bottom.

Aug 25

Sept 10

Gravel Grow Cups – Light Usage

Indoors, light definitely matters with growing plants and it is also true with gravel. The experts cite that for ideal growth distance your lighting needs to be six inches away from the plant. Although ideal, often lights are much farther away. With gravel, if you have lights close on the plant, the leaves will develop broader. If you have light farther away, the stem of the plant will be longer.

An example of this can be shown with the cucumbers below. On the left the cucumbers (a) had closer light, on the right with cucumbers (b) the light was a few feet away. After 12 days the cucumber plant with the closer light has a shorter stem and now entering into its second leaf development, whereas the cucumber with the light farther away is taller and not in its second leaf development. Shorter growth with wider leaf structures is more ideal for growth.

Cucumbers (b)

Cucumbers (a)

With the pea shoots below, light angles also matter. As shown, the pea shoots are tilting towards the lights. With growth being ¼ inch to 1-inches a day depending on the plant type, a poorly angled light event for a few days can have an adverse impact on plant development. Ideally, light is directly above the plant and closer on the plant.

Pea Shoots

Gravel Grow Cup – Transplant and Repeat

Photo 1 below depicts cucumbers in a gravel grow cup that are ready to transplant. Photos 2 to 4 show the process of taking the contents out of the cup, gravel first, then the sand with the plant roots. By now the roots have grown into the sand. Sand is also sedimentary so roots can live in sand. Photo 5 illustrates the separation of the seedling roots within the sand, where in photo 6, the cucumber seedlings are separated and ready to transplant. Rinse and wash out the cup. Put the sand back into the cup and then the gravel. You may notice less sand in the cup due to the sand attaching to the roots. You may need to put additional sand in the cup before adding gravel.

Gravel Grow Cup – Transplant and Repeat

Photo 1 to the left shows micro greens that have run their course, started to decay and are ready to empty and start over. Photo 2 depicts the same cup after the roots and micro greens have been cleaned out and replaced. Photos 3 to 6 display the process of pouring out the contents, gravel first then the sand and roots. In photo 7, the sand, gravel and roots are separated. Rinse the cup and then you can start over by pouring back in the sand and then the gravel displayed in photo 8. Feel free to plant other seeds in the center of the gravel. Once you have the new seeds in the cup and you've placed the cup on the drip tray, water to the top and watch the process repeat itself.

Transplanting

On this page, we will walk through the process of transplanting from a small growing area designed to germinate and grow seedlings to individual soil-based containers for continued growth. Below, we see beans that have been growing and producing beans for a few weeks in gravel ideal for transplant. With the amount of gravitational energy along with expanding roots, most plants will ultimately die out due to lack of space. It is best to transplant to an outdoor environment. You can also have transplant shock solution to dip the roots in to help with the transplanting process. Here we did not have those items. Because roots are fragile and rocks are hard, it is likely better to transplant to soil.

To transplant individual seedlings, you first must prepare the destination location. We are transplanting into a larger soil-based location. There are two transplant options. Option A: Take out loose gravel from the top until you reach the roots. Then squeeze the cup to loosen the sand and gravel. Pour the entire contents into soil (sand, gravel and roots). Then cover with soil and water. This method is ideal if your roots are interconnected with other roots as is the case below with these multiple bean sprouts.

Option B: Pour out the cup of gravel and carefully disentangle the root system and plant the root sprouts in soil. This is ideal for those single seed sprouts as is the case with the bean sprout below. See a visual of this process below. Despite the transplanting steps below, gravel gardening is best done outdoors where roots can travel laterally without space restraint.

Option A

1. Start with your existing sprouts.

2. Slowly squeeze the entire contents to soil-based destination hole.

3. Stand up gravel/sand base in the soil and cover with the soil.

Option B

1. Start with your existing sprouts.

2. Slowly squeeze the entire contents out on a flat surface.

3. Carefully separate roots.

4. Plant roots 3 to 4 inches deep and cover with soil.

53

Gravel Grow Cup - Soil vs. Rock

The images below depict the growing competition between three river rock samples and soil; all in gravel grow cups. The river rock samples include rock from the Patuxent River, rock sold at Ace Hardware, and rocks gathered at the Outer Banks in North Carolina. Pea shoots and wheatgrass seeds placed in each cup demonstrate the reaction in each growing environment. After 15 days the gravel-grown pea gravel was three times the height of soil-grown pea gravel. The quality of pea shoots differed in that the fresh river rock (i.e., Patuxent and Outer Banks river rock) appeared sturdier than the Ace Hardware-bought rock. At the 25th day the soil-grown pea gravel had caught up. For the wheatgrass each growing environment grew the wheatgrass at the same rate.

Patuxent, Ace, Outer Banks, Soil

Pea Shoots

Wheatgrass

Pea Shoots

Wheatgrass

Gravel Grow Bottle

In the spirit of research and development, the science of geological agriculture expanded to create the gravel grow bottle. Theoretically, since gravel feeds water with nutrients, it is likely that gravel placed at the bottom of a water bottle should feed the water so that it can support plant root structures. The ideal plants for the gravel grow bottles are 5- to 10-inch stemmed plants that grew previously in a gravel grow cup. A string bean seedling growing in a gravel grow cup was placed in the gravel grow bottle with a hanger trellis below on March 1. Squash plants transplanted to a gravel grow bottle on March 1 sustained the plant to March 15, when the plant entered its flowering pod phase (see below). The squash grew for about another three weeks before it began to die. Not all plants are suited for the gravel grow bottle. Bulb plants will not work as the bulb is too large to fit in the hole at the top of the water bottle.

String Beans – March 1

String Beans – March 1

String Beans – March 1

Squash – March 1

Squash – March 13

Squash – March 15

Gravel Grow Bottle

On March 3, 2016, plants that grew in a gravel grow cup found a home in gravel grow bottles. Each plant seedling was carefully removed from the gravel grow cup and placed in the gravel grow bottle, making sure the roots were suspended in the water with the leaf serving to keep the plant outside the bottle. Squash, cucumbers, string beans, pea shoots and cucumbers became the test seedlings for the gravel grow bottles.

The root images to the right depict the root system of the string beans on April 7 when the plant had evolved to its flowering stage. The root structure on the bottom right of the lima beans on April 7 illustrate a decaying and discoloration of the rock. This suggests that some plant roots may have adverse reactions to the gravel grow bottle while others may thrive.

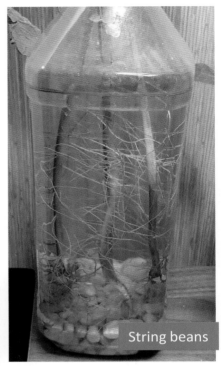

String beans

Squash

Cucumbers

String beans

Pea Shoots

Lima Beans

Squash

Gravel Grow Bottle – String Beans

The string beans seemed to adapt well enough to produce a few full beans in the gravel grow bottle. From its initial placement in the gravel grow bottle on March 3, the image on April 3 shows the plant entering its pod stage. Four days later the new bean emerged. One month later, the same plant grew its third bean as shown on May 5. The back wall was needed to hold the plant upright while it grew in the gravel grow bottle. Shown on the prior page, the root systems

expanded well in the gravel grow bottle, crawling along the walls of the bottle. Normal CFL lights used in the growing of this plant enabled sustainment in the micro-farm. In addition to the fact that the bean actually grew to full term, the second most important aspect of the gravel bottle configuration is water conservation. Adding ½ cup of water once every two weeks seemed to provide suitable water for plant sustainment.

April 3

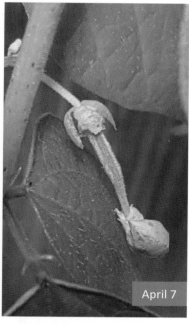

April 7

April 19

May 5

May 5

Gravel Grow Bottle – Pea Shoots

These pea shoots below, transplanted in the gravel grow bottle on March 3, grew on a basement windowsill. These photos, taken on May 3, two month later, show that the pea shoot grew about 30 inches. In a gravel grow cup, pea shoots can grow at an inch per day but in the gravel grow bottle, the plant grew about a half-inch per day. Even though the plant grew long in the bottle, the roots crawling along the walls of the bottle appear short. The dark pea shoot seed is visible with the plant's stalk going up and its roots surviving over two months in this water-only ecosystem fed by sedimentary rock or, in this case, Ace Hardware store-bought river pea gravel. This approach also lends itself to recycling water bottles, as these bottles are best suited for this type of plant sustainment with gravel.

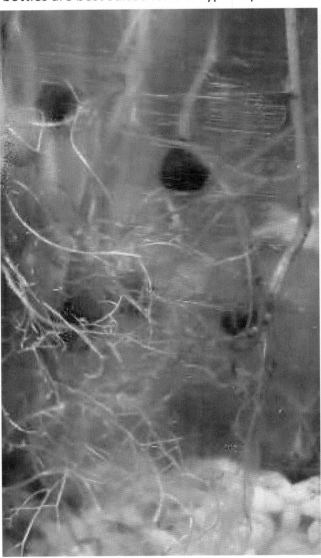

Gravel Grow Bottle – Cucumbers

The cucumber seedlings transplanted into a gravel grow bottle on March 3 and examined again on May 15 depict the evolution of cucumber seedling plants in the gravel grow bottle. As shown, cucumbers appear to do well, maturing to their flowering stage while displaying multiple flowers. Despite the apparent success, the cucumber plant did not produce a cucumber in the bottle as witnessed earlier with the string beans. The roots of the cucumbers in the gravel grow bottle also behaved differently than string bean and pea shoot roots. The cucumber roots grew what appears to be algae on its root structure in the gravel grow bottle as seen below. It is currently unknown why the roots behave in this manner with cucumbers than with the string beans and pea shoots, but the answer likely rests in the fact that roots secrete various type of enzymes when growing. It is possible that the enzymes being secreted by the cucumber roots are amplifying algae buildup.

It is necessary to note that cucumbers do not produce actual cucumbers in the gravel grow cup either. In the gravel grow cup, the cucumber plant also grows to the flowering stage but does not progress much further. Only in the outdoor gravel gardens so far have cucumber plants grown to full term in gravel as shared in the outdoor section of this book.

Windowsill Gravel Gardening

In 2014, a winter gardening initiative was piloted at Ace Hardware in Takoma Park, MD, on the store's windowsill. With most gardening efforts halting in the winter, gravel enables indoor gardening year round. Arranging gravel grow cups indoors in the winter provide ongoing access to nutrition, especially with micro greens, sprouts, beans and peas, which tend to grow to full term in the gravel grow cup.

Given the nutritional value and quick growing performance of micro greens and sprouts in gravel, ongoing check-ups and watering is recommended. Once plants are active, they will require watering two or three times per week. Gravel grow cups can last about 60 to 120 days before the roots crowd the plant and you need to start over.

Plants shown here are after two weeks and the micro greens and sprouts are ready for harvest.

Bean Mix

Peas

Marigolds

Cucumbers

Wheatgrass

Sunflowers

Plants on this page ready for harvest after two weeks include bean mix, wheatgrass, alfalfa, savory mix and sunflower sprouts.

Bean Mix, Alfalfa, Savory Mix, Wheat Grass, Peas, Sunflowers, Cucumbers and Marigolds

Indoor Gravel Micro-Farm

The photos below depict the indoor gravel desktop micro-farm or small growing operation with multiple edible plants. About $30 of supplies, mostly in seed cost, produces a wide variety of plants growing inside this basement during the winter. Several recycled containers along with the standard 9-ounce gravel grow cup enables each plant to live in its own space. In the top image, marigolds, squash, lettuce, corn, pea shoots, iris, scallions, dill, cosmos, cucumbers, oregano, gladiola and spinach make up the micro-farm. All plants were seeded within 21 days of taking the top photo below.

Although many of these types of plants will need more space, not all do. The flowering plants can be situated for aesthetic purposes around the house. The spices, sprouts, micro greens, lettuce and spinach are edible after one inch of growth. Obviously, some plants perform better after a few more weeks, but many are already edible. The corn, squash and cucumbers are the few plants that truly need transplanting. The lettuce will need thinning. Some plants will thin naturally. Ultimately all plants grow better outdoors but with good light, water and space management, a permanent indoor farming system for these plant types provides year-round access to nutrition.

The photo to the left shows the indoor desk micro-farm of tomorrow arranged to its maximum growing space by using the space under the table. With a few lights and a few bins, you can set up a small efficient growing space in a back room indoors. The primary challenge is managing the growth a few weeks later and at that point, thin, eat or transplant.

Indoor Gravel Micro-Farm

The indoor gravel micro-farm below in the basement of a homeowner illustrates how a back tool room can be converted to a 100% organic micro-farm for about $30. One bag of gravel can support about 65 gravel grow cups. This basement farming operation has a half-dozen to a dozen gravel grow cups per seed type. This approach provides enough nutrition per plant type where should one cup of wheatgrass be harvested on the first day and reseeded, and then move to the next cup the next day and reseed, one would have permanent daily access to wheatgrass as long as the homeowner continues to reseed after each use. One seed pack can last a year or longer per gravel grow cup.

Oct 11

Sept 27

Oct 8

Oct 10

Oct 11

Oct 22

Indoor Gravel Micro-Farm

The indoor gravel micro-farming techniques are ideal for a wide variety of plant types. From lettuce, cilantro and alfalfa sprouts that grow like a bush, to pea sheet and bean mix that grow like weeds, access to green space is a stone's throw away. The thing to remember is that gravel grows. Therefore it will always produce potassium, silica and copper when wet and so will your plant. Active indoor gravel gardens will need daily check-ups for optimal use and benefit.

What Grows in the Gravel Grow Cup?

The Gravel Grow Cup – Plant Expectation Matrix below shares the observed outcome of 40 seed types, planted in the gravel grow cup. Key notes that are not intuitive: 1) With seed quantity, plant one or any amount up to what is listed. 2) Although transplanting is not required with some plants, feel free to transplant any plant. 3) Bush growth style are plants that are edible where you can snack on them once they are a few inches high. 4) Y-micro means that the plant will grow in the gravel grow cup but it will be a micro version compared to how the plant typically grows.

GRAVEL GROW CUP - PLANT EXPECTATION MATRIX

Seed Type	Seed Size	Seed Quantity	Seeding Location	Trellis Needed	Trellis Height (inches)	Plant Height (inches)	Plant Growth Style	Time to harvest or move (weeks)	Harvest period (weeks)	Full term in GGC?	Transplant required?
Common Crops											
Arugula	Small	20 - 30	Top	No		2	Bush	6 to 8	2 to 3	Y - micro	No
Beans	Medium	8 to 12	Center	Yes	18 to 24	18 to 24	Stemmed plant	6 to 8	2 to 3	Yes	No
Broccoli	Small	20 to 30	Center	No		6	Stemmed plant	6 to 8	2 to 3	No	Yes
Cherry tomatoes	Tiny	10 to 20	Center	Yes	6 to 12	6 to 12	Stemmed plant	6 to 8	2 to 3	No	Yes
Corn	Medium	5 to 10	Center	No		6	Stemmed plant	6 to 8	2 to 3	No	Yes
Cucumbers	Medium	5 to 10	Center	Yes	6 to 12	6 to 12	Stemmed plant	6 to 8	2 to 3	No	Yes
Edemame	Medium	5 to 10	Center	Yes	10 to 16	10 to 16	Stemmed plant	6 to 8	2 to 3	No	Yes
Lettuce	Tiny	30 to 40	Center	No		2 to 3	Bush	6 to 8	2 to 3	Y - micro	No
Okra	Medium	5 to 10	Center	Yes	6 to 12	6 to 12	Stemmed plant	6 to 8	2 to 3	No	Yes
Peas	Medium	5 to 10	Center	Yes	8 to 16	8 to 16	Stemmed plant	6 to 8	2 to 3	Yes	No
Spinach	Small	30 to 40	Top	No		2 to 3	Bush	6 to 8	2 to 3	Y - micro	No
Squash	Medium	5 to 10	Center	Yes	6 to 12	6 to 12	Stemmed plant	6 to 8	2 to 3	No	Yes
Sunflowers	Medium	10 to 20	Center	No		6	Stemmed plant	6 to 8	2 to 3	No	Yes
Tomatoes	Small	10 to 20	Top	Yes	6 to 12	6 to 12	Stemmed plant	6 to 8	2 to 3	No	Yes
Spices											
Basil	Small	20 to 30	Top	No		2 to 3	Bush	6 to 8	2 to 3	Y - micro	No
Cilantro	Medium	20 to 30	Center	No		2 to 4	Bush	3 to 8	2 to 3	Yes	No
Dill	Tiny	20 to 30	Top	No		2 to 4	Bush	6 to 8	2 to 3	Y - micro	Yes
Garlic	Tiny	20 to 30	Center	No		3 to 6	Thin	10 to 12	2 to 3	Y-micro	Yes
Oregano	Tiny	30 to 40	Top	No		1 to 2	Bush	8 to 12	2 to 3	No	No
Parsley	Medium	20 to 30	Center	No		3 to 6	Bush	6 to 8	2 to 3	Yes	No
Scallions	Tiny	20 to 30	Center	No		2 to 4	Thin	4 to 8	2 to 3	Y - micro	Yes
Micro Greens & Sprouts											
Alfalfa Sprout	Small	30 to 40	Top	No		2 to 3	Bush	2 to 3	2 to 3	Yes	No
Bean Mix	Medium	30 to 40	Center	No		6 to 12	Weed - like	1 to 3	2 to 3	Yes	No
Broccoli Sprouts	Small	30 to 40	Top	No		2 to 4	Bush	2 to 3	2 to 3	Yes	No
Fenugreek	Medium	10 to 20	Center	No		2 to 4	Bush	2 to 3	2 to 3	Yes	No
Pea Shoot	Medium	10 to 20	Center	Yes	18 to 24	18 to 24	Weed - like	1 to 3	2 to 3	Yes	No
Sunflower sprouts	Medium	10 to 20	Center	No		6 to 10	Stemmed plant	2 to 3	2 to 3	Yes	No
Wheatgrass	Small	30 to 40	Center	No		5 to 8	Grass	1 to 3	2 to 3	Yes	No
Bulbs & Flowers											
Begonia	Large	1	Bottom	No		5 to 10	broad leaf	8 to 12	2 to 3	No	Yes
Cosmos	Small	10 to 20	Center	No		5 to 10	Flower	6 to 8	2 to 3	Y - micro	No
Gladiolus	Large	1	Bottom	Yes	36 to 42	24 to 48	Tall spike	8 to 12	2 to 3	No	Yes
Hyacinth	Large	1	Bottom	No		5 to 8	Flowering bulb	6 to 8	2 to 3	Y - micro	No
Iris	Large	1	Bottom	No		8 to 16	Tall spike	8 to 12	2 to 3	No	Yes
Marigolds	Medium	10 to 20	Center	No		4 to 8	Stemmed plant	8 to 12	2 to 3	Yes	No
Tulips	Large	1	Bottom	No		2 to 4	Flowering bulb	6 to 8	2 to 3	Y - micro	No
Zinnias	Medium	10 to 20	Center	No		4 to 8	Stemmed plant	8 to 12	2 to 3	Yes	No
Fruit											
Watermelon	Medium	5 to 10	Center	Yes	12 to 24	4 to 8	Stemmed plant	6 to 8	2 to 3	No	Yes
Cantelope	Medium	5 to 10	Center	Yes	12 to 24	4 to 8	Stemmed plant	6 to 8	2 to 3	No	Yes
House Plants											
Aloe	NA	1	Low center	No		8 to 16	Long limbs	32 to 48		Yes	No
Jade	NA	1	Low center	No		5 to 10	Slow	52+		Yes	No

Chapter 2 Summary

Chapter 2 reviews a variety of indoor configurations for setting up gravel growing environments. These configurations aim to assist users in developing an understanding of how to take everyday items and repurpose for nutrition access at home. A broad range of plants appears to grow well in gravel-based ecosystems from common crops such as beans and peas to micro greens and sprouts like wheatgrass and pea shoots. Ideal methods for efficient gravel growing configurations indoors include but are not limited to the following:

Gravel Grow Cup – The gravel grow cup is a self-contained small growing container using sand and gravel as the primary growing ingredients. The sand at the bottom of the cup regulates water passage into the cup while the gravel atop the sand releases nutrient material for plants to grow. Ideal cups have 25% sand and 75% gravel. The cup requires tiny drainage holes on the bottom for water access and tiny air holes on the sides to allow the ecosystem to breathe. A required drip tray serves as the water storage reservoir. Seeds placed halfway in the gravel layers of the cup tend to germinate and grow when water is added to the cup.

Recycled Gravel Gardens – Plastic recycled containers provide the perfect space for gravel gardening as the plastic material allows users to puncture the tiny holes needed for water and air. Ceramic pots and glass vases are not designed for the insertion of tiny holes, making recycled containers better suited for indoor gravel gardens. The basic sand-gravel configuration, 25% of the space with sand on the bottom and 75% of the space with gravel on top, applies to recycled containers as well. Once seeded and watered, plants tend to grow.

Gravel Grow Bottle – The gravel grow bottle configuration uses a recycled water bottle, with rocks at the bottom, as the complete growing environment for seedlings. The bottle configuration requires users to add gravel to the bottle so that 25% of the water bottle has gravel at the bottom. By filling water to the top of the bottle, the gravel will leach nutrient material into the water for root sustainment – hence the gravel grow bottle.

Gravel Micro-Farming - A gravel micro-farm is a small indoor growing area where a wide variety of edible plants grow for household consumption. Typical micro-farming areas are basements, atop tables in a small room or inside a closet. A six-foot table can hold and grow up to 70 gravel grow cups.

Winter Gardening – Gravel enables consumers to garden during the winter indoors in a clean and efficient cost-effective manner, providing access to fresh nutrition during cold months.

Plant Expectations Matrix – This "indoor" matrix shares the observational summary of how the listed plant types tend to grow in a gravel grow cup using CFL lights in a temperature-controlled environment. The growth pattern in soil is not the same as the growth pattern in gravel. Additionally, the growth pattern in the indoor gravel grow cup is not the same as the plant's growth pattern in an outdoor gravel garden.

Chapter 3
Outdoor Gravel Gardens

Outdoor Gravel Garden Introduction

The outdoor gravel gardens are very similar to the indoor gravel growing activity. The basic similarity is that the gravel is the growing environment and the sand is used as the irrigation regulator. There are, however, several key configuration differences between the gravel grow cup indoors and gravel gardens outdoors. This chapter will explore 20 years of gravel gardening experiences outdoors. Gravel gardening overall grew out of an outdoor accident. Consequently, much of the initial research is outdoors. It wasn't until 2014 did the indoor applications emerge due largely to the Lowell School in Washington, DC, where gravel evolved into a classroom gardening special projects experiment for 3- and 4-year-old kids.

The chapter begins in 2011 with the first Washington DC-base gravel garden. As shared in this chapter, the first step in answering uncle Logan's question included recreating a similar growing environment in Washington, DC. The list of supplies provides the overview for how the outdoor application differs from indoors. The six-year observational study includes the gardens moving from one house to another as the family moved from Washington, DC, to Ellicott City, MD.

The outdoor chapter continues with gravel growing activity at the Lowell School and Yu Ying Elementary School in Washington DC, and at various single-family homes in Washington DC, as well as Ace Hardware in Takoma Park, MD. The observational study at these locations covers a four- to six-year growing period depending on location. The goal of the study period is to demonstrate the durability and cost-effectiveness of gravel gardens.

The chapter continues with a look at how uncle Logan's gardens are doing after 20 years of organic accumulation within his gravel beds. Additional outdoor applications explore how to configure gravel gardens on cement and how to survive off of gravel gardens when lost at sea or in outdoor pots.

Outdoor gravel gardens provide a variety of benefits when set correctly. Once a gravel garden is assembled properly outdoors, homeowners and apartment dwellers will not have to add anything to the garden for years to come except seeds and water. Weeding reduces significantly, and there is no need for fertilizers. Rainwater is sufficient to sustain the garden with no manual watering required except when first assembled. Properly configured gravel gardens are drought resistant so that during 100 degree-plus days plants tend not to die.

The goal of the outdoor chapter of gravel gardening is to equip users with the knowledge to create a personal gravel garden of any size anywhere in the world. This chapter shares test results for over 40 seed and plant types for their reaction with gravel-growing environments outdoors. With over 100,000 seed types on the planet, much more observational research is required.

Gravel Gardening Materials

The primary materials needed to create an outdoor gravel growing environment are:

1. **River pea gravel (rivers stones)**
2. **Sand**
3. **Cotton-based lawn fabric**
4. **Plastic**

The pea gravel should be from rivers, oceans or lakes, generally referred to as *river pea gravel*. The sizes range from 3/8 of an inch to 2 to 3 inches. Buy the 3/8-inch river pea gravel when purchasing for your outdoor gravel garden. The larger rocks don't work as well, as the root systems tends to catch better with the smaller river pea gravel. There are many types of river pea gravel. During your first year, you should test multiple types of locally available river pea gravel to determine which type works best in your climate. It only takes 2 to 4 weeks to test the viability of river pea gravel. Buy only one bag and see what works against what you are trying to grow. See photos above for the best brand of pea gravel tested to date and found at retail stores. The Kolorscape brand of pea gravel found at Ace Hardware and other hardware stores tends to be a reliable brand for crop production.

The **sand** should be beach-like play sand with tiny particles of rock similar to what is found on the beach. This type of sand is common in most locations that sell sand. **Do not**, however, use powdery sand or sand that sticks to your hand upon touch. **Do not** use colored sand. Sand represents the water storage reservoir used to maintain moisture for a sustained period of time. Sand retains and releases water, while soil absorbs and consumes, enabling sand to act as an underground water storage facility.

The plastic can be plastic rolls or recycled plastic. Photo 1 shows an example of plastic in a roll. There are two types of lawn fabric needed, the gray industrial type and the black cotton cloth garden type (see photos 2 and 3 below). The black cloth is referred to as the capillary fabric as it carries water along the surface of the fabric. The gray fabric will retain water longer so that water is held for use in the gravel gardening system. **Do not** use the plastic-based lawn fabrics as plastic placed above the sand neither retains nor carries water. Ultimately, the gray industrial fabric retains water while the black lawn fabric carries water to the gravel and eventually to the root systems.

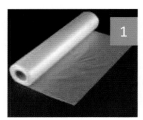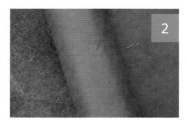

Gravel Testing and Lettuce - 2011

Before converting large areas into gravel gardens, test a variety of locally available river rock. The photos below demonstrate the testing prior to showing the steps to configuring your outdoor gravel bed. In the test gravel garden below, the dimensions are 2 feet by 4 feet by 1 inch deep of gravel. Four types of gravel competed with lettuce and marigolds serving as the test seeds for the experiment. Type A, C and D gravel came from a national retail chain. Type B gravel came from Tennessee. The Tennessee gravel is the gravel type that we have used most in our 20-year study of this process. Grass seed was planted in Type D to assess grass growth characteristics in gravel. Ten days later the first lettuce sprouts led the way for lettuce on the table 60 days after planting (March 27 to May 25). Here, one inch of gravel sustained the lettuce growing cycle. As you can see below, type B gravel lettuce is doing better than the other two types. Type B is the Tennessee gravel. The variability of gravel types demonstrates that you should test the various gravel types in your area before settling on a specific gravel type. Although it seems that type A gravel is less capable than type B gravel, most of the plants described in this manual grew in type A gravel sold at Ace Hardware. Home Depot sell type C and D gravel.

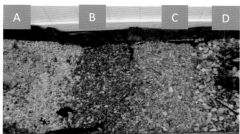

April 3, 2011

April 10, 2011

Lettuce and Marigolds, May 3, 2011

Lettuce, May 3, 2011

Lettuce, May 17, 2011

Lettuce, May 25, 2011

There are six basic steps in setting up your outdoor gravel garden:

1.   Prepare the site
2.   Dig the trench
3.   Lay the plastic and fabric
4.   Lay the sand
5.   Lay the gravel
6.   Plant the seeds

Trench

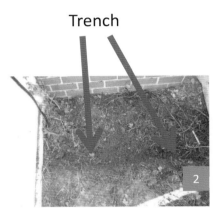

Step 1 – Prepare the Site

Identify and clear the outside area where you plan to have your garden. The areas should be flat and receive good sunlight for at least six hours a day. You can choose a raised bed or an in-ground bed as shown in photo 1. Sloped areas are not as effective, as the moisture become uneven. All things considered in-ground beds tend to perform better because the roots are underground and are better protected against weather fluctuations.

Step 2 – Dig the Trench

Dig a 6- to 10-inch deep trench along the center of the identified garden area. **The trench should run along the longest side of the garden down the center**. For example, with a 3-foot wide by 6-foot long garden space, the trench should run along the center of the 6-foot length. An ideal trench can range from 6 to 10 inches. See photo 2 for the trench placement. As you see, the top of the trench tapers off (see photo 3). Tapering the top some allows the sand to flow more evenly across the material. The key step is to dig a good trench. You can also spray weed kill on this cleared area to kill off any deep-rooted weed roots. Weed spray is optional. The diagram to the right is similar to the photos, except in the diagram it shows the gravel fully underground. In the photo version, we simply added gravel and then put up a brick retaining walls as a barrier. The illustration is provided to show a cross section of how it looks underground with the trench and gravel.

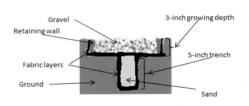

Setting up Your Gravel Garden – The Trench

Outdoor gravel gardens require a good sand trench to maintain the proper moisture level so that the gravel's nutrient materials can feed root systems. Without a proper trench, moisture is not sustained and nutrients are not leached from the rock. Recognize that water held in the sand trench can only travel so far. We recommend a maximum of four feet on either side of the trench for an even and sustainable moisture distribution in the gravel system. Any longer than four feet may cause the moisture to dry up faster, reducing the chances for a sustained moisture level in the gravel. We also recommend having the gravel depth a maximum of six inches high as the water moisture can only travel up the rocks so far. Should you lay a foot or more of gravel, moisture control adjustments may help keep the system moist.

Below, we have several shapes that represent a variety of garden shapes with the dimensions listed in feet. The brown area represents the gardening area while the beige lines the sand trench. In all cases, you lay the two fabric types prior to pouring the sand in the trench. Remember, the trench represents the water storage reservoir for the gravel garden and that any distance past four feet may be too long a distance for the water to travel for a sustainable moisture level.

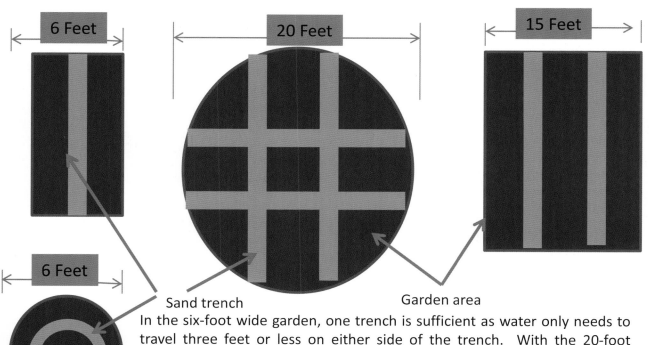

Sand trench

Garden area

In the six-foot wide garden, one trench is sufficient as water only needs to travel three feet or less on either side of the trench. With the 20-foot circular garden, we recommend the grid like a tick-tack-toe configuration to ensure moisture coverage throughout. The 15-foot wide garden has two long sand trenches. This configuration should enable good consistent moisture. When watering, you want to flood the gravel bed, allowing the water to recede into the sand trench, storing water for future use.

Step 3 – Lay the Plastic and Fabric

Cut enough of both types of lawn fabric so that it covers the entire area. Lay plastic then the gray industrial lawn fabric first so that both cover the entire area and into the trench. The plastic and fabric retains water, but eventually allows water to soak through and drain (see photo 1).

Next, lay the black cloth lawn fabric on top of the gray fabric so that the black fabric is in the trench as well. The capillary nature of the black fabric will carry water to everywhere it is laid (see photo 2).

Step 4 – Lay the Sand

Pour sand into the trench so that it completely fills the trench to the top. Wipe the sand so that it is flat. The sand can taper off at the top. Next, cover the sand with a strip of the black fabric. This will allow the capillary nature of the sand to spread the water evenly onto the black lawn fabric (see photos 3 & 4).

You may insert a 12-by-2 inch PVC pipe at one end of the sand to provide water directly to the sand. The water goes directly to the sand in this case. **You do not have to insert the pipe, as water can easily flow to the sand with normal rain watering** (see photos 3 & 4). The pipe is used only when trying to conserve water or delivering special materials to the gravel bed. In a drought, you can water the pipe only to sustain moisture in the system and conserve water.

Setting up your gravel garden

Step 5 – Lay the Gravel

In this 4-foot by 4-foot space, we sought to lay a three-inch deep gravel bed. This area required four bags of gravel weighing 50 pounds each of river pea gravel bought from a local nursery (see photo 1). The final step is to spread the gravel evenly over the fabric in the enclosed area. In this case, we used a brick border (see photo 2).

Step 6 – Plant the Seeds

Next, plant seeds either on the bottom of the gravel bed or half way down. Seeding one inches or less would put the seed in the dry zone and it would likely not germinate. In your first year, seed liberally to see how the seeds take to your specific type of gravel. We call abundant seeding "gravel juicing." The upper growing limits of a gravel garden is unknown so feel free to add many seeds to determine the growing patterns.

In photo 1, tomatoes, carrots, cucumbers and broccoli seeds represented the first test seeds. By seeding halfway though or about 1 ½ inches down, the seeds have the opportunity to grow. If seeds are planted ½ inch in the gravel garden, the seed will dry up and die. The top inch of the gravel garden is the dry layer.

Watering

When you first set up your gravel garden outdoors, water until it floods. Water twice a week for the first three weeks. After that water weekly. If it rains often you shouldn't need to water much.

Home Gravel Garden Cycle - 2011

As the months went on, over 100 cucumbers and about 20 tomatoes grew from the 4-foot by 4-foot gravel garden. Most of the tomatoes were eaten by squirrels or fell before picking. The carrots only grew as deep as the gravel, or three inches. Although we did make certain cuts in the fabric to accommodate the carrots, we obviously did not cut in the proper places. By September, the cucumbers' vines had begun to decay and decompose back into the gravel, adding organic material and nutrients to the gravel bed, which tends to strengthen output the next year. Even worms have begun to find refuge in the gravel, suggesting a good, nutrient-rich environment. With a gravel nutrient source, these tomato roots grew shorter than normal as roots tend not have to travel as far in seek of food and nutrients.

July 2011	July 2011
September 2011	October 2011
December 2011	December 2011
January 2012	January 2012

Home Gravel Garden Cycle - Cucumbers - 2011

The lifecycle of cucumbers in a 4-foot by 4-foot by 2.5-inch deep gravel garden is shown below. Sprouts start relatively well after about 11 days with the first cucumbers arriving in about 60 days (May 3 to July 2). Other crops planted and grew in this space (carrots, tomatoes and broccoli) for testing purposes, but the cucumbers dominated. During this period, we only watered 5-times for the entire season. Although it rained, the temperature was in the mid-90s for most of July and the gravel-grown cucumbers thrived while our soil-based crops died in the heat. The cucumbers were later tested and the results depict near identical measurements of nutrient value as USDA-approved cucumbers. The funnel pipe is visible in the beginning, but later it was not needed as the rain provided the periodic water necessary while the coolness beneath the rocks kept the water stored longer for root growth and sustainment.

Cucumbers, May 14, 2011 - 11 days after planting

May 14, 2011 - the first sprouts can be seen

Cucumbers and tomatoes, June 1, 2011

Cucumbers, June 17, 2011

First Cucumbers, July 2, 2011

Cucumbers, August 2, 2011

Home Gravel Garden Cycle - 2012

Photo A below illustrates the remaining vines after the first season. Remove non-composted vines by hand, clear debris, and plant new seeds. Ground settling tends to reduce gravel depths, requiring an additional bag or two in the second season to maintain the 2.5-inch depth. Photo C represents sprouts one month after planting from seed, but it was a cold spring so growth slowed. Photo D depicts growth after two months of tomatoes, scallions, spinach and cherry tomatoes. Plants growing well included: scallions on the lower left; spinach (down the row in the center) and tomatoes (back wall and right wall). Photo E shows volunteer tomatoes that returned from the previous year. There are about 15 tomato plants that sprouted from tomatoes that fell last November. In photo F, the spinach was ready to cut and was cleaned and put on a plate. In photo D, the tomatoes on the left wall started in 2012, while the back wall tomatoes returned from the 2011 planting and appear much larger.

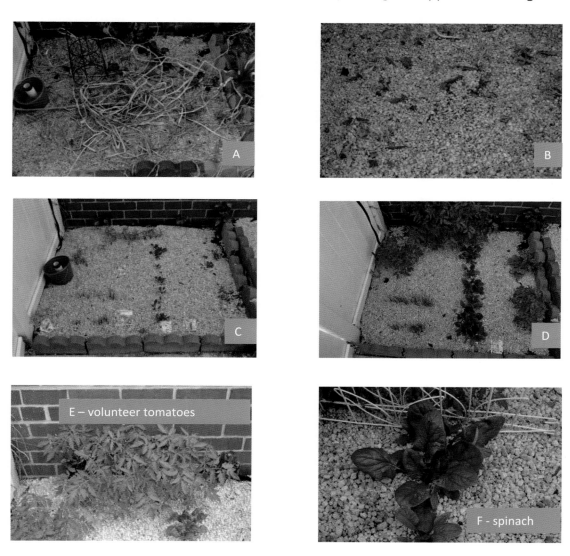

In 2012, an additional space enabled the development of a second gravel garden. Photo A depicts the original 4-foot by 4-foot garden, featured on the prior pages. A new 4-foot by 7-foot gravel garden complemented the existing gravel bed. In photo B, a plastic trash bag serves as the first retaining layer, extending the water storage capacity of the sand for longer use in the gravel system. Photo C shares the two layers of fabric that serve as the underpinning of the gravel bed. Photo D illustrates five bags (250 lbs.) of sand in the trench. Finally, photos E and F highlight the final step: laying the gravel.

Home Gravel Garden Cycle - 2012

Photo A depicts the original 4 x 4-foot garden on the left, plus the new area constructed in 2012. Corn and cucumbers planted in the new 4 x 7 foot area in late April provided crops by July. Photo B, taken in June, shows the tomatoes, scallions and corn. Photo C shows the corn near maturity in mid July. As the corn died, photo D, taken in September, shows the ongoing tomatoes and cucumbers. By late October, photo E illustrates tomatoes still going, while the leaves of corn and cucumbers begin to decay back into the gravel ecosystem. Photo F, taken in December, depicts the gravel garden at the end of the 2012 season when most of the vegetation decayed to enrich the gravel garden next season. The auto-composting effect adds organic material to the gravel bed after each growing cycle .

April 2012

June 2012

July 2012

September 2012

October 2012

December 2012

Home Gravel Garden Cycle - 2013

In 2013, this gravel garden entered its third year. As shown, good emergence occurred by early May with the lettuce ready for harvest by early June. By July the garden's squash, beans and cucumbers provided food for the dinner table. Shortly after, the cherry tomatoes came, generating about 500 cherry tomatoes from July to early November. Pumpkins and watermelons also grew in the gravel garden this year. Similarly to 2012, plant leaves and vines decayed back into the gravel garden at the end of the season.

May 7, 2013

June 5, 2013

July 8, 2013

July 8, 2013

October 4, 2013

November 9, 2013

Home Gravel Garden Cycle - 2014

In 2014, the gravel garden was in its fourth year and volunteer cherry tomatoes began returning from the 2013 season. About 50 cherry tomato plants came up, producing over 1,500 cherry tomatoes in 2014. Another 100 fell to the ground and decayed prior to picking. The tomatoes' harvest period began in July and ended in October.   Beans, lettuce and peas grew to full term throughout the season. The beans produced for about four rounds of crops from June to August. At the end of the season the remaining vines, leaves and unpicked crops decayed back into the gravel growing ecosystem.

March 22, 2014

May 29, 2014

July 24, 2014

July 24, 2014

August 2, 2014

October 20, 2014

Home Gravel Garden Cycle - 2015

In 2015, the home gravel garden was in its fifth year. In April, remaining leaves and vines that didn't decompose were removed and new seeds were planted. Cherry tomatoes returned naturally as the tomatoes that fell in 2014 reseeded the gravel garden. Other crops planted in 2015 include beans and peas. The corn grew but not as well as in prior years. The scallions returned from being planted from seed in 2013. A volunteer lettuce leaf demonstrates that lettuce may occasionally volunteer in gravel. By now, this gravel garden is said to be fully sustainable for tomatoes, where each year a robust crop of tomatoes will come without any manual seeding, fertilizing or watering.

April 5, 2015

May 14, 2015

Tomatoes - May 14, 2015

Corn - May 14, 2015

Lettuce - May 14, 2015

June 2, 2015

Home Gravel Garden Cycle - 2015

During 2015, the harvest of tomatoes, beans and peas provided a good crop for the kids. The tomatoes produced from July through November while the beans provided about three cycles of ongoing beans from May to August. The peas usually produced about two cycles of pea pods. Logan, our vegetarian, loved eating right out of the garden.

June 1, 2015

June 10, 2015

Tomatoes – June 17, 2015

Tomatoes – June 17, 2015

Tomatoes ready – July 29, 2015

Cherry tomato harvest – August 28, 2015

Fallen tomatoes – December 12, 2015

Cherry tomatoes – flowering December 12

83

Home Gravel Garden Cycle - 2016

In 2016, the family moved. The gravel garden below was in its sixth year and saw its last planting of string beans, gladiolus, pea, along with the remaining volunteer cherry tomatoes that returned each year. The images below depict the growth cycle from May 1 to June 8 and includes outdoor newcomer edamame, which opened up that plant for ongoing planting.

The success of indoor edamame plants in gravel grow cups during the winter led to trying this delicious plant outdoors. The photo below in the center displays the edamame flower bloom that advances the coming of the actual edamame pod. The pods were never picked as the move prevented access during the height of the edamame pod phase.

Gladiolus

Cherry Tomatoes

Edamame

Edamame

The scallions of the previous year returned and grew well. The taste and smell was particularly strong and the micro scallion bulb that grew possessed a strong taste. This unexpected return volunteer can be a great spring surprise to a garden.

A variety of plants volunteer well in gravel, meaning that they tend to return the following year, whether you want them to or not. Scallions, marigolds, tomatoes and occasionally lettuce can return each year when growing in gravel. The mum plant also returns well the following year. Plants that return year after year are referred to "plant sustainable" where you seed once and the plant returns for years without the need to manually seed again. Cherry tomatoes and marigolds are good examples.

Home Gravel Garden – 2015 – Tulips

During the fall of 2014, tulip bulbs found a home at the bottom of a gravel garden. As you can see below, the tulips did pretty well by the spring of 2015, even being transplanted inside the home and surviving for a week to 10 days after transplant. Despite success with tulips here, tulip bulbs and gravel can be hit or miss. Sometimes, shallow planting can lead to squirrels digging up the bulbs. In other circumstances, bulbs decay before they "hatch." Further study is required on why some bulbs do well like below, and other do not.

November 25, 2014

November 25, 2014

March 21, 2015

April 13, 2015

April 18, 2015

Home Gravel Garden – 2015 - Begonias

This home gravel garden, in its second year, is shown with store-bought potted begonias and petunias planted on May 1, 2015. The tulips from earlier in the season are still visible in the top photo. Corn seeds planted on May 1 grew to a degree.

May 5

On May 5, the begonias seemed to have acclimated to the gravel environment. The soil root is visible due to the shallow nature of this gravel garden. Ideally, potted plants are completely submerged in gravel.

June 28

By June 28, as shown here, the begonias were still vibrant, but the petunia flowers seemed to die out. The corn grew and wheat grass planted a week earlier was about three inches high.

July 17

By July 17, the begonias were still looking good. The petunia flowers returned and the wheat grass was bushy, 12 inches high and harvestable long ago.

Potted petunias were planted on May 1, 2015. The top photo below was taken on May 7 and shows tulips growing in the background. The bottom photo, taken on July 12, shows how petunias react to gravel. These flowers died by late August. In growing petunias in soil, they seem to grow wider. Gravel does seem to sustain petunias for a few months.

Home Gravel Garden Cycle - 2017

This home garden grew sunflowers, gladiolus, lettuce and arugula in the summer of 2016, providing an array of fine crops. Planted initially on May 1, the May 15 photo illustrates the plant height at two weeks while the July 8 photo shows where each plant began filling out. Both the lettuce and arugula grew into harvestable salads and the gladiola flowers bloomed. The arugula also entered its flowering stage by July 5; one can harvest arugula seeds if so informed on the seed harvesting methodology.

This garden grew a great assortment of popular plants during the period, providing both food and visual floral plants.

Home Gravel Garden Cycle – Sunflower

The sunflowers grew well over the observation period. Notice the height at the center July 16 photo well above six feet with the gravel depth being only three inches. Also notice the number of stalks on the top right-hand photo. Gravel is able to support a wide number of seeds in a small growing area, providing enough nutrients to sustain a range of complex plants.

June 2

July 16

July 16

July 16

July 30

July 30

Home Gravel Garden Cycle - 2017

From July 30 to August 30 the sunflower plant transitioned from a vibrant bee-attracting flower to actual sunflower seeds. Bees enjoyed the sunflower plant and seem to enjoy most gravel-grown plant flowers. The images below depict the evolution of the sunflower plant. The near 10-inch sunflower provided thousands of sunflower seeds for family enjoyment. About 17 sunflower plants grew in the small space.

July 30

July 30

July 30

July 30

August 15

August 30

August 30

The sunflower seed harvesting process below beautifully shows how sunflower seeds are removed from sunflower plants and bagged. Only one of the three sunflower plants were harvested and bagged, demonstrating the amount of sunflower seeds that could be produced in the small space. The largest sunflower plant provided enough sunflower seeds to fill three quart-sized bags.

Home Gravel Garden Cycle – Marigolds – 2011

Although planted at the same time in 2011, the marigolds ran a much longer course than the lettuce. It took about 90 days for the initial marigold flowers to bloom. From June to November the number of marigold flowers grew strong and robust, providing six months of marigold flowers for the bees and backyard. By December, when the first frost started, the marigolds began to die and decompose.

With gravel-growing environments, the cold weather has a more adverse impact than with soil. With rocks being open and this gravel bed being one inch deep, cold weather easily passes through the rocks to freeze plant roots. In soil, an inch below the surface remains relatively warm so roots can last longer. During the first few weeks of December, the temperature dropped below freezing at night and killed the marigold roots, leading to the drastic change from the height of bloom in November to the decaying process settling in during December. Despite cold effects, it appears that each gravel type successfully grew marigolds. There does seem to be some slight color differences in the marigolds along the three gravel types where planted, which suggests that each gravel type may have a different effect on the type of crop grown. The finer details of the various effects of various gravel types is unknown to be studied by academic institutions.

April 28, 2011

May 12, 2011

June 25, 2011

August 10, 2011

November 17, 2011

December 14, 2011

Home Gravel Garden Cycle – Marigolds – 2012

In early June 2012, volunteer marigolds returned from the previous year as shown in photo A. In mid-September, gardeners accidently put mulch over the gravel bed. As seen in photo B, the number of flowers were few. In late-October, the marigold flowers expanded with many bees abuzz depicted in photos C and D. Photo E shows how much more robust the marigolds grew in one month, but photo F shows how big the marigold flowers grew before the frost. It appears that the mulch over gravel may aid the gravel gardening ecosystem. Mulch helps trap moisture so it likely aides in moisture retention which is ideal for gravel beds. This bed is also 1-inch deep so moisture support is likely beneficial.

June 1, 2012

September 28, 2012

October 26, 2012

October 26, 2012

October 26, 2012

November 24, 2012

94

Home Gravel Garden Cycle – Marigolds – 2013

In 2013, the marigolds returned naturally for the third year in a row. Seeds from 2012 fell and germinated. They grew up to four feet in 2013 but broke after a storm hit. The bees loved the gravel-fed marigolds. Mulch is also mixed in this gravel bed. At the end of the season, over 500 harvested seed pods provided the inventory to seed almost an acre of land. There are about 100 seeds in each pod, or an estimated 5,000 total seeds.

July 27, 2013

October 6, 2013

October 6, 2013

October 6, 2013

October 17, 2013

January 10, 2014

In 2014, the marigolds came back naturally for the fourth year in a row. Seeds from 2013 fell and germinated. This year, however, lima bean seeds replaced marigolds in the right side of the gravel garden. As you see in the July, September and October photos, both the marigolds and lima beans did well for several months. The first round of lima beans harvested in late-July led to a second round harvested in October. As in prior years, the marigolds grew to full bloom after July, flowering through mid-November.

July 14, 2014	August 3, 2014
September 29, 2014	October 15, 2014
October 15, 2014	November 17, 2014

Home Gravel Garden Cycle – Marigolds – 2015

In 2015, the marigolds came back naturally for the fifth year in a row. Seeds from 2014 fell and germinated. We did pick about 500 seed pods again at the end of 2014. These pictures go only through May 14, 2015, but already show a variety of marigold plants coming back, with about nine good plants. Based on prior years, this type of start in 2015 should yield a bounty of marvelous marigolds.

As the 2015 summer continued, the marigolds once again grew bushy, reaching about three feet tall, flowering continuously from July to mid December, now five years since the first seeding. This garden is said to be marigold-sustainable where you no longer need to seed and marigolds will return annually.

Home Gravel Garden – 2016 - Sunflowers

This large pot is also in its fifth year of growing plants with gravel. This year gladiola bulbs began growing after two weeks as shown on May 15. By June 2 the spikes were well developed and by July 5 the gladiola flower was in full bloom.

Flowers lasted until the end of July. Although gladiolus grow tall in the gravel grow cup they do not flower in the gravel grow cup. Only outdoors will gladiolus flower in gravel gardens. A trellis is ideal when growing a gladiola in gravel. Another option is to plant gladiola deeper, which means developing or configuring your gravel bed 4 to 6 inches for the purposes of gladiola growing. The next few pages share additional gladiolus grown in 2016.

May 15, 2016

June 2, 2016

July 5, 2016

July 5, 2016

July 10, 2016

The gladiolus flowers on top are from the Ace Hardware gravel garden in Takoma Park, MD. The gladiolus below are from a home gravel garden. Each set of tested gladiolus plants grew and bloomed into a beautiful flower.

Home Gravel Garden – 2016 - Gladiolus

The coral colored gladiolus below demonstrates that gravel can produce a range of vibrant colors of all tones consistent with the bulbs; in this case gladiolus. Not all bulbs do this well in gravel but this species of gladiola bulbs seem to enjoy the gravel environment. Additional tests across the spectrum of bulb species will provide clarity on expected performance going forward.

The gravel grow pots below grew beans and peas. Being reliable and usable plant types the concurrent growth rate enables both to pod simultaneously so that both vegetables are enjoyed together. Beans and peas are very reliable plants with indoor gravel grow cups, where they grow tall up to 24 inches.

Outdoors both peas and beans can grow tall or short depending on whether or not the pot is assembled with a trellis. Under the sun, peas can grow up to four feet tall while the beans can climb up a trellis up to five or six feet tall.

The time from germination to full beans or peas outdoors is about five to six weeks. Similarly, the indoor gravel grow cups mature beans and peas over the same period of time. The outdoor plants, however, yield greater crops of beans and peas when grown in gravel, providing a decent crop for an ongoing side dish for dinner. The indoor gravel grown beans and peas will provide a few beans for snacking.

Nutrition – Pea Shoots

According to www.peashoots.com, pea shoot are considered a super food, boasting seven times more vitamin C than blueberries, eight times more folic acid than bean sprouts and four times more vitamin A than tomatoes. As a reference, vitamin C is a powerful antioxidant that helps to protect the body from free radicals. Vitamin A from beta-carotene is important for the skin and helps keep the immune system healthy. Folic acid, known as folate in its natural form, is one of the B-group of vitamins. It is needed to make healthy cells and blood.

Gravel does particularly well with pea shoots. According to the packaging, pea shoots take about 10 to 20 days to mature to the one- or two-inch height level. Indoors, pea shoots grow an inch per day maxing out at 36 inches. Outdoors, after the four-foot mark, the pea shoots start flowering, yielding fresh pea pods. Photos below depict the purple flower and how Logan loves to eat pea shoots right out of the cup.

Pea Shoots – 3 Feet

Pea Shoots – Pods

Pea Shoots – Flowers

Eating Pea Shoots

Home Gravel Garden – 2016 – Front-yard

In 2016, the Campbell family moved to their home in Ellicott City, MD. The photos below outline the gravel garden construction process from start to finish. The gravel and sand itself came from the family's previous home in Washington DC, in large garbage bins. Consistent with prior configurations, step one is to dig the proper trench. Step 2 is to lay the plastic over the growing area and into the trench, and then lay the lawn fabric over the plastic into the trench. Step 3 is to pour sand into the trench and cover the lawn fabric over the sand. Finally, step 4 is to pour the gravel into the gravel bed. This gravel is considered "six-season gravel" as it possesses six seasons of prior plant organic decay, building up six years of new organic material. Worms participated each year of the decaying process, providing new fresh organic soil each season. Gravel gardens age like fine wines, improving slightly each year.

There are two types of gravel being assembled in this gravel garden. The gravel on the right comes from the Washington, DC, gravel garden that came from Ace Hardware six years ago with tomato spores within.

The rock on the left is a mix of aged Tennessee river rock and aged Ace Hardware rock.

Home Gravel Garden – 2016– Front-yard

Pea shoots, cucumbers, lettuce, tomatoes and beans began growing on July 30. By August 9 the pea shoots and cucumbers provided green bookends to the gravel garden. The first consumption by Logan of the pea shoots on August 19 shows how robust pea shoots grow outside. Based on the appearance of the pea shoot bush, consider the pea shoots' nutritional value and what that nutritional value could provide to someone who does not have access to proper nutrition. Typical of prior gravel gardens, by September the cucumbers were much taller than they were previously and they continued growing well after the pea shoots died out. The volunteer tomatoes emerged and the beans also produced to full term.

July 30

August 9 – Pea shoots and Cucumbers

August 19 – Peas Shoots

September 1 – Lettuce and Cucumbers

September 12 - Beans

September 27 – Tomatoes, Lettuce, Cucumbers

Home Gravel Garden – 2017 – Backyard

In 2017, the gravel in this garden entered its seventh season of crop production. The April 26 photo demonstrates how many beans can grow in a small space outdoors. Two other new plants that demonstrated success in 2017 include parsley, which grew into a significant bush, and grass to demonstrate the ability for gravel to grow grass for lawns and cow feed.

April 5

May 27

April 26 - Beans

July 27

September 10- Parsley

April 26 - Beans

July 27 - Grass

Home Gravel Garden – 2017 – Backyard

Once gravel gardening techniques begin to provide crops for the household, some choose to add more beds on the property. In 2017, a 4 x 6 foot gravel garden replaced a quarry gravel area. Installed in the backyard, the construction processes followed the standard steps of land clearing, trench digging, plastic and fabric laying, sand pouring, covering and adding gravel. Typical of outdoor gravel gardens, peas, string beans and gladiolus grew first, requiring a trellis after the first month.

Home Gravel Garden – 2017 – Backyard

by June 3, 2017, the peas flowered, and by June 17 produced harvestable peas consistent with prior growing patterns. The other seeds planted in this garden did not grow, as they were the previous year's seeds. Additional seeds planted on June 15 included squash, cherry tomatoes and cantaloupe.

June 1 - Peas

June 3 - Peas

June 17 - Peas

June 17 - Peas

June 17 - Peas

June 17

June 17

Home Gravel Garden – 2017 – Backyard

As the peas died watermelon, cantaloupe, tomatoes and squash seeds grew. By August 14 the harvestable squash enjoyed fine dining on the dinner table. The visible cherry tomatoes preparing to turn green added comfort that a strong tomato bounty was forthcoming. The tomato plant itself grew to 7 ½ feet tall in only three inches of gravel.

June 23

July 26

August 14

July 26

August 14

August 14

Home Gravel Garden – 2017 – Backyard

A trellis was added to this outdoor gravel garden to help control traffic within the gravel growing environment. In prior years the plants tend to mix up, so adding a trellis provides a convenient space and helps guide the growth vertically. The trellis itself is chicken coop wire cut into a trellis tube. The plants growth up, with the vines climbing on each ladder of the trellis. The tomatoes grew eight feet tall while the squash plant grew five feet tall.

Cherry Tomatoes

Cantaloupe

Marijuana

Squash

Cherry Tomatoes

A key feature of this particular gravel garden is that each plant has a metal chicken coop wire arranged into a trellis tube, guiding the growth of the plants.

Each plant is able to grow vertically, climbing up the chicken wire. The squash plant is five feet tall while the tomato plant outgrew the eight-foot trellis. The cantaloupe to the right inside a trellis tube climbs up with cantaloupes in tow.

The weight of the tomato plant caused the addition of the tiki torch to help hold the chicken wire in place. In previous gravel gardens, the lack of trellis support created a gravel forest of several plant types intertwined with one another. The trellis tube here helps control growth traffic in small spaces, sending plants up, not out.

With a taller trellis this 8 foot tomato plant may get to 10 or 12 feet. Notice the plant is almost to the second floor of the house.

Oliver Home Gravel Garden – 2013

The two lettuce types below grew in a local home garden in 2013 at the home of Stephen and Erica Oliver in Washington, DC. Both the arugula and lettuce grew fairly large into December of 2013.

Mix Greens

Lettuce

Oliver Home Gravel Garden – Weeding 2014

In the gravel gardens shown so far, weeding was not an issue with the fabric and plastic serving as a barrier under the gravel. The weeds that do emerge come from airborne spores that fly and land on the gravel bed.

With the Oliver gravel garden, the garden is situated next to a grass lawn. When mowed the lawn cuttings of the lawn flew into the garden several times from March to June. As seen in the first photo taken in July, the airborne grass has significantly taken root in the garden to the point that the homeowner had to de-weed the gravel garden.

Photo 2 depicts how the grass roots grew in the gravel. These roots run across the lawn fabric and can over-run the garden. A metal rake assists in weeding gravel gardens. It is recommended to strike the rocks hard where you find the weeds to help loosen the roots that have attached to the fabric.

Photo 3 of the garden after the de-weeding process became the second season garden for the family.

To avoid airborne grass from cuttings, gardeners can put up a barrier screen fence, quickly blow off any fallen grass blades or use capture bags when mowing.

Oliver Home Gravel Garden – 2014

After de-weeding, the Olivers planted a variety of crops at the end of July, including the items shown here as well as peas, cucumbers and okra. Aside from the photo take in August, the rest were taken on September 28. The Olivers ate out of their gravel garden from mid-September to late-November. This late-season garden shows that with gravel, you can seed in late-July and still yield a great crop the same season. This second-year gravel garden also has a season of organic decay to aid in the process.

Lettuce

August

September

Zucchini

Tomatoes

Winter Squash

Yellow Squash

This okra plant (or really a tree) grew well in the Oliver gravel garden. As you can see, the okra itself is the size of your hand, much larger than what you may find in the stores. This particular okra plant grew five feet tall and produced okra continuously from late-September to the first frost in December. The height of this okra plant coupled with the size of the trunk as shown along with the manner in which this okra was seeded illustrates a phenomenon that is often observed in gravel gardening called *gravel grafting*.

Gravel grafting is the theory that when you plant certain seeds in gravel, as they germinate, they graft or merge together to form a larger-than-normal plant heart to yield a larger-than-normal plant with greater yields. We often plant many seeds but get a huge single plant instead of many plants. Conversely, for some seeds like beans, if you plant 20, you will get 20 bean plants.

Oliver Home Gravel Garden – Okra – 2015

This okra plant grew well in the Oliver gravel garden. This photo was taken in the spring of 2015 where the six-foot tall plant now has seeds for reseeding this season.

Okra Seeds

Oliver Home Gravel Garden – 2015

Arugula

Dill

The 2015 garden started with leftover three-foot tall dill and arugula and then matured later in the summer with tomatoes, cantaloupes, squash, cucumbers and other items.

Cantaloupes

Tomatoes

In 2017, poor lawn mowing practices sprayed the Oliver gravel garden with grass cuttings multiple times. After the first good rain the gravel garden became a gravel grass growing or hay growing operation. The grass in the gravel grew faster and taller than soil-grown grass. A lawnmower used to cut the "gravel lawn" revealed that lawnmowers could cut a gravel-grown lawn without operational issues. Based on how the lawnmower took to the task, it was easily able to mow gravel-grown grass. This grass test validates that gravel could actually support lawns in areas like San Antonio and New Mexico stricken with poor soil quality. Gravel is also suitable to cultivate and grow grass for cow feed and hay for horse feed.

Impatiens purchased from Home Depot were planted at the Howard family gravel garden, where a hole was dug in the gravel and the entire contents of the pot were placed in the hole and then covered with gravel so that none of the soil was exposed. You may need to add gravel to your bed if the contents of the pot are deeper than the gravel bed. Planted pots can be 4 to 10 inches tall, so if you plan to plant potted plants in gravel, be sure to account for the depth of the gravel bed.

The impatiens shown in photo 1 were planted on July 24. They sustained themselves for over three months as photo 2 was taken on September 26.

When planting potted plants in gravel, it is recommended that you water the soil directly for the first few weeks every other day. This will aid in the process of the roots separating from the soil and expanding and sustaining itself in the gravel ecosystem.

Impatiens

Potted Transplanting – Tulips and Pansy

Below we have gravel-grown tulips being transplanted to a front porch pot of gravel. Also in the same pot is a pansy bought at Home Depot. Tulips only last a few days and each closed tulip opened in gravel and lasted for about one week in gravel. The pansy, however, took root on April 20 with one flower and had about five flowers on May 14 with about four visible plants on the way. Even indoors as shown below, the tulips that were taken from the backyard gravel garden lasted a week indoors. All of the bulbs below were grown in gravel and transplanted to another gravel-growing environment.

April 10, 2015

April 10, 2015

April 26, 2015

May 14, 2015

April 13

April 13

April 14

April 17

April 20

120

Lowell School Gravel Garden – 2012

March 15, 2012, marked the date of the first elementary school playground gravel garden construction (photo E). Students participated, watching the digging of the trench, the laying of the fabric, sand and gravel, and then the seeding. Due to a cold April that year, the first attractive lettuce sighting on growth May 1 (photo F) encouraged teachers and students. By May 18 the lettuce had been harvested once (photo H). Although the lettuce made it through the cold season, the other seeds stalled until the weather warmed. Gravel is not good in the cold because it allows more cold air to affect the plant roots. These seeds began showing growth once the temperature increased. Photo H depicts corn, cucumbers and marigold plants emerging and acclimating to the gravel growing ecosystem.

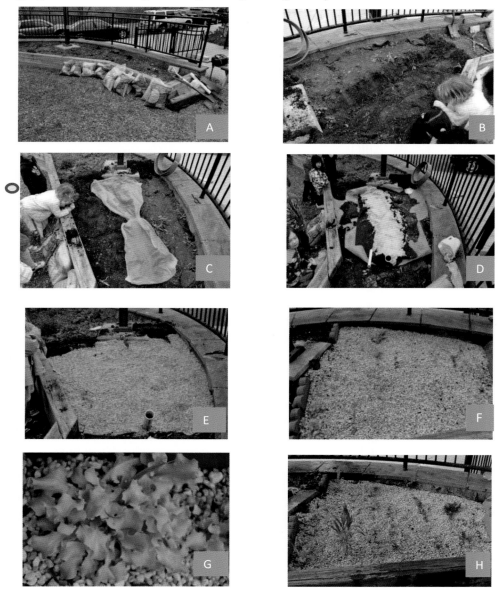

Lowell School Gravel Garden – 2012

Photo A, taken on May 19, shows the corn coming in. Students had already harvested once by this point. In early June, photo B depicts the corn gaining ground and the marigolds forming on the right. The lettuce had been harvested five times by mid-June. Also in photo C, you will notice an expanded gravel garden area. Flowers were planted in this new area. By mid-July, the corn and cucumbers are ready to pick as shown in photo C. Someone even took a bite of the corn and it was really sweet and juicy. Photo D shows the corn dying out by mid-July, but the corn and cucumbers were still going. By August in photo E, the corn was dead and the cucumbers began fading. The marigolds and other flowers were doing well. Up until October as seen in photo E, the flowers were doing well and a volunteer cherry tomato plant was ready for harvest. You can see a little red tomato on the vine.

Lowell School Gravel Garden – 2013

The Lowell School gravel garden produced a harvest for the kids for the second year in 2013. Photos show that by mid-May, the kids were able to eat lettuce snacks in between playing on the playground and class. By July, the summer school camp kids were able to snack on corn and cucumbers while seeing beautiful gladiolus growing nearby.

April 17, 2013

May 16, 2013

July 8, 2013

July 8, 2013

July 3, 2013

July 3, 2013

Lowell School Gravel Garden – 2014

In its third year, the Lowell School gravel garden grew squash and added sunflowers to its line up of crops. A few zinnias also returned from the previous year. In October, pea shoot sprouts were planted and excited the kids. The photo shown in October depicts Logan picking pea shoots out of the garden and eating them on the spot. The sweet taste of the pea shoot seeds from Botanical Interests has led to the winter windowsill gravel grow snack program where kids grow pea shoots in the gravel grow cups and snack off the windowsill through the winter.

Squash
July 11, 2014

Zinnia
September 1, 2014

Squash
July 11, 2014

Sunflower
September 1, 2014

Pea Sprouts
October 24, 2014

124

Lowell School Gravel Garden – 2014

July was a good month at the school gravel garden as squash, corn and beans were harvested for the summer camp kids. July 29, as shown, was a good day for produce from this garden. Being adjacent to the playground, kids are able to enjoy the gravel garden while at play.

July 10, 2014

July 29, 2014

July 29, 2014

July 29, 2014

July 29, 2014

July 29, 2014

Lowell School Gravel Garden – 2015

In 2015 the Lowell School gravel garden was now four years old. This season micro greens and sprouts were planted on the far right, with cucumbers, beans and corn seeds in the center and various flowers on the left side of the gravel bed.

April 20, 2015

Broccoli sprouts, bean mix, pea shoots

April 20, 2015

June 6, 2015

Beans and cucumbers

June 6, 2015

Flowers, common crops, sprouts

September 5, 2015

Beans and cucumber

September 5, 2015

Corn

September 5, 2015

Lowell School Gravel Garden – 2015

All photos below were taken on September 5, 2015, at the Lowell School gravel garden.

Scallions

Sunflower

Broccoli sprouts

Flower

Beans

Zinnia

Lowell School Gravel Garden – 2016

The Sweet Williams flower and onions retuned from the prior year. Gladiola and lettuce planted on April 15 already demonstrated a good start by May 7.

Lettuce

Onions

Gladiolus

Sweet Williams

Sweet Williams

Sweet Williams

Sweet Williams

Lowell School Gravel Garden – 2017

By June 8, the Lowell School gravel garden onions and gladiolus developed into attractive green space visuals for preschool kids. While the Sweet William flower began to die out the Asiatic lily was starting to open it's colored blooms.

By September 1, the sunflower bloomed bright under the sun, promising sunflower seeds to students during the school year.

Onions

Lily

Sunflower

Sunflower

Gladiolus

Gravel does well with tulip bulbs as shown below. These photos where taken at Lowell School, where kids planted the bulbs in the fall. Unlike bulbs planted in soil that come back each year, bulbs planted in gravel tend to die out after one use. The primary factors for why gravel is less sustaining on bulbs than soil are insulation and wildlife. In soil, bulbs are deep in the ground and kept at a constant temperature. In gravel, the cold can freeze out the bulbs. In cinder blocks the bulbs seem to be insulated enough to complete a full cycle once, but the following year, the bulbs will likely not produce. Wildlife also affects bulbs in gravel. We find that squirrels dig up bulbs in gravel from time to time while in soil this is more difficult. Because of this, the school conducts annual bulb planting in the fall with the kids.

Lowell School Gravel Garden – Tulips - 2014

The second year of the fall tulip planting for the kindergarten classes led to the spring tulips shown below. This kicks off what the students may plant in the spring. In other research and observations, some tulips will return when the bulbs are planted in deeper gravel gardens of four inches or more. A degree of insulation is provided so that cold weather and squirrels don't affect the bulbs. In the configuration below, tulips will need to be planted annually. In the school environment, this provides an annual activity for each incoming kindergarten class to witness the gravel growth cycle with tulips.

Lowell Micro Greens and Sprouts - 2014

With warm weather in October, micro greens and sprouts were planted in advance of an open house. The ideal temperature for gravel gardens is 60 degrees and above. These outdoor micro greens and sprouts illustrate the ability to quickly grow fresh, nutritious produce in just a few weeks. The wheatgrass, broccoli sprouts and bean mix below are all edibles.

October 24, 2014

October 10, 2014

October 24, 2014

October 10, 2014

October 24, 2014

October 10, 2014

October 24, 2014

132

Yu Ying School Gravel Garden - 2014

The Yu Ying Public Charter School in Washington, DC, planted a gravel garden in May 2014, dropping seeds of cucumbers, squash, beans, lettuce, zinnias and corn. By July, the lettuce, beans, cucumbers and squash were ready to pick. The corn didn't do well. The garden club created a nice sign to distinguish the gravel garden with the soil garden also at the school. When this garden was installed, students would take the rocks and throw them. To prevent this, chicken wire was placed on the garden to prevent rocks from being taken. This is ideal for public places. The plants will likely grow and fruit above the protective wire.

June 6, 2014

June 6, 2014

June 16, 2014

June 16, 2014

July 18, 2014

July 18, 2014

As shown, the gravel garden has evolved from producing vegetables in the summer to flowers in the fall. Because of this, it is ideal to plant some flowers with vegetables.

August 23, 2014

August 23, 2014

August 23, 2014

August 23, 2014

November 3, 2014

Uncle Logan Home Gravel Garden - 2010

Uncle Logan has been applying gravel gardening techniques since the inception of the notion that rocks could feed root systems. The next few pages depict photos from the Logan garden in 2010 and 2014, most producing plants and crops since 1998.

Here we have Swiss chard and iceberg lettuce growing in trash cans that are lined with plastic. We conserve water by putting a funnel pipe directly into the sand. At small home gardens you can water easily. When you have large planting spaces, you can save water by directly watering the funnel pipes. Here the gravel is about three inches deep, with the sand six inches deep and soil filler at the bottom. The plastic is placed over the soil but under the sand and gravel.

Swiss Chard

Here we have a 20 x 8 foot x 4 inch deep gravel bed. The trench runs along the center of the 20 feet so that the water feeding distance between the trench and the edge of the bed is four feet on either side. Here we have green beans growing on the fence as shown. With this configuration, water is added through the funnel pipe as shown in the garbage can version above. These photos were taken in August 2010 so the beans have already peaked.

Beans

In this large 20-foot circular gravel garden, we have asparagus and elephant ear plants growing. You see the water hose here. This was done to make it easier to water. Simply place the hoses appropriately and water as necessary. When constructing a bed of this type, one needs to dig trenches in a grid format or a circular format so that the trench is dug in a way that allows the water to only have to go four feet in either direction. With asparagus roots, you need to place them in the sand trench, then add about three inches of gravel. We have fencing around this bed to protect against local wildlife.

Asparagus

Here we have a 10 x 10 foot raised bed with cinder blocks as the barrier and protective fencing. You can use any type of barrier, as most use wood or plastic barriers to raise the bed. In a similar fashion with raised beds, you create the area, dig the trench using either the single long row or grid, lay the plastic and then fabric, and then pour the sand and add the gravel. The use of cinder blocks makes the structure durable. This gravel bed was constructed in 1998. This photo of what is left of the year's strawberries was taken in 2010.

Strawberries

In this gravel garden, we have not changed the bed nor gravel in 12 years and have never added fertilizers.

Swiss Chard

Cinder blocks can also be used as planting pods as well where you line the bottom of the space with the plastic, then fabric, then sand, and finally gravel. Here we have Swiss chard growing. You can also see the PVC funnel pipe used in this instance to provide water to the sand trench beneath the gravel. The raised bed is 8 x 12 feet. This bed is actually on a platform. With this type, you add 6 to 10 inches of dirt on the base before laying the fabric. The addition of dirt allows the trench to exist above ground. This is done to create a large bowl effect so there is little water loss.

These golden squash leaves are climbing up the fencing. This 6 x 10 foot gravel bed was constructed in 1999, with these photos of the 2010 crop. Incidentally, this was after a 55-day drought in Tennessee, the location of this gravel garden. Despite the lack of rain, the underground capillary watering system kept the gravel cool and moist throughout the drought. In this case, the funnel pipe was critical to the large planting operation to conserve water.

Squash

Uncle Logan Home Gravel Garden - 2014

The Logan aged gravel beds in TN, are now 15 to 20 years old, accumulating over a decade of decay and composting, annually improving the growing ecosystem of the gravel gardens. The photos on this page were taken in October 2014. The bounty of potatoes and tomatoes (or French fries and ketchup as some say) as shown in photo 1, depicts a larger than normal potato. The five-foot tall marigolds are a visual delight, producing thousands of seed pods for next season. The sweet potatoes in photo 3 often come in groups of two or three as shown.

Uncle Logan Gravel Garden – 2014 – Okra

Dubbed "Jumbo Gumbo," this 12-foot okra plant (or tree) has reached new heights. Despite the blurred image, 8- to 10-inch okra can be seen growing. You will definitely need a ladder on this one.

The Logan gravel gardens are the oldest gravel gardens in the world. Some of the gravel beds are 10-year enriched with some up to 20 years of annual enrichment or appreciation. The natural organic appreciation coupled with the natural characteristics of the gravel creates growing environments in which you may get a 12-foot tall okra plant or five-foot tall orange daisies.

A well-seeded gravel gardening environment can provide the homeowner with crops and attractive vegetation from March to December.

The longer you have a gravel garden, the better it will produce. Ironically, those with active gravel gardens often face the challenge of harvesting what grows. As you can see here, it is unlikely that all of the available okra will be picked this year, as only two people live at this home.

Gravel Boring

This year, we noticed that Mother Nature always finds a way with gravel gardening. The natural growth within the gravel bed is constantly expanding roots. As roots crawl along the fabric, they tend to bore through the fabric to the soil underneath, referred to as *gravel boring*. This is of course if you did not place plastic under the fabric when you constructed the gravel bed. Should you construct your gravel garden without plastic, where you have the fabric as the only barrier between the gravel and the soil, then the roots of your plants that are growing in gravel will bore through the fabric into the soil. What can happen next may surprise you depending on what you are growing.

The best example of this can be shown below. Here we see a sweet potato that is being harvested. The roots, however, are also attached to a sweet potato that has grown in the soil underneath the fabric. These sweet potatoes enjoyed the benefits of the gravel and the soil. The soil underneath a gravel bed set up in this nature (without plastic) will likely be more fertile than soil that has not had the benefit of constant concentrated gravel nutrients passing through it. As you can see, the sweet potatoes are pretty large, consuming the entire hand.

If you are lucky to have experienced gravel boring with a range of crop types from potatoes to carrots or other in-ground crops, you will have to cut the fabric to extract the crop underneath. As you do this, you should place a fabric patch over the area that you cut. Otherwise, the root systems will mix with the soil (which is not necessarily bad) and can cause weeds to emerge from beneath. It remains to be seen if crops that are gravel fed but bred in soil have any nutritional difference, but an examination of gravel boring may prove interesting.

Sweet Potatoes

Deep Pit Gravel Gardens - Tomatoes

Uncle Logan experimented with a deep pit gravel garden in 2014 with tomatoes. To construct it, he dug a 4 x 4 foot x 5 foot deep hole. The next step is to line the hole with fabric so that the fabric covers all of the exposed soil. Next, pour down about one foot of sand so that the entire area at the bottom has the same one-foot depth of sand. Cover the sand with lawn fabric. Next, pour four feet of gravel into the pit to the top. Then, drop in a small plant or seeds. Finally, fill the pit with water once to the very top.

The deep pit gravel garden was created to allow the tomato roots to grow downward, which is their natural tendency rather than across as is the case with more shallow gravel gardens. The result, as you see, is basically a 10-foot tall tomato tree, fruiting like an apple tree. By allowing the roots to run deep in gravel, the plant tends to grow bigger, stronger and better.

Gravel Gardening on Cement

"Can gravel gardens do well on cement?" is a common question posed when considering urban and rooftop applications for geological agriculture. The answer is both yes and no. The underbelly of the gravel garden must be kept cool for the gravel ecosystem to function properly. Constructed on soil, the Earth provides a natural cooling base for the gravel garden which helps keep water in the system longer and enables trace condensation to occur on really hot days.

If you want to configure a gravel garden on a rooftop, deck or cement patio, you will have to elevate the gravel so that the underbelly of the gravel ecosystem remains cool on hot days. An example is provided on the following pages. A more crude method is also shown, which was constructed out of recycled materials including an old mattress. As long as you elevate the underbelly of the gravel bed off of the cement, then the answer is yes, you can build a gravel garden on cement.

Cement can heat up to 100 degrees and burn everything from beneath in one day. If you construct a gravel garden directly on cement, then on a hot day, the cement will heat the underbelly of the gravel bed and kill all of the crops in one day. Never construct a gravel garden directly on cement. If you construct a gravel garden on cement, then the answer is no, gravel gardens do not do well on cement.

Gravel Gardening on Cement

The image to the right is a raised gravel garden on an old mattress. The lining of an SUV hatchback serves as the basic "container" of the gravel bed. Under the two inches of gravel is a layer of fabric, two inches of sand, a supporting layer of fabric with a layer of plastic underneath. Tomatoes, beans, cucumbers and zinnias seeds planted on June first matured by August 15.

The beans and zinnia grew to full harvest. The tomatoes in the back developed some but only produced one cherry tomato. The cucumbers started but did not finish. With the in-ground gravel bed, the tomatoes grew well during the same period, further suggesting that in-ground gravel beds may perform better as they likely retain more moisture.

This is not ideal but it does demonstrate that elevating gravel on cement is recommended. The heat of the summer did not burn the bottom of the gravel bed this time around.

Zinnia, beans, tomatoes, cucumbers

Beans

Zinnia

Building Gravel Gardens on Cement - 2014

Gravel gardening on cement requires gardeners to raise the garden off of the cement so that the cement does not burn up the underbelly of the gravel garden on hot days. To do so, as shown in photo 1, place concrete retaining wall bricks to outline the desired growing area. Next, place support bricks and blocks through the interior of the area spaced a foot apart. Photo 2 depicts two wood boards that have been placed on the retaining wall bricks. This board becomes the bottom support structure of the gravel garden. Feel free to treat and weatherize the board for longer use. Next, place plastic over the board and another layer of retaining wall bricks as seen in photo 3. Next, fill in the area with organic materials such as leaves, grass cuttings, hay or soil (photo 4). Place plastic over the organic material then commercial lawn fabric over the interior area (photos 5 and 6). With a degree of insulation serving as the underbelly, place sand in the interior, then lay lawn fabric (photos 7 and 8). Next, put in a few larger river rocks before adding the normal 3/8 inch of rock. Finally, add a final layer of retaining wall bricks and fill the gravel to the top so that you have at least 3 to 4 inches of gravel. Now your gravel garden is ready for planting either seeds or pre-existing plants. Potted mums and micro green seeds were planted as shown in photo 11.

Building Gravel Gardens on Cement - 2014

The raised gravel bed below was a late season gravel garden planted only on September 1 with transplanted potted mums with sunflower sprouts, mix beans and wheat grass planted from seed. The mums started orange, faded to yellow by September 15, with the flowers dying out by September 29. The leaves stuck around and new flowering buds emerged by late October in burgundy with the mums coming back to the original orange by November 17, almost three months after planting. Since no one was around to harvest the sunflower sprouts, they grew to budding, nearing the flowering stage as shown on November 2, but as the temperature dropped, the flowering process stalled. The wheat grass and bean mix also grew to about three inches high and stayed at that level as the cold came.

September 15, 2014

September 29, 2014

October 31, 2014

November 2, 2014

November 17, 2014

November 17, 2014

Gravel Gardens on Cement – 2015 Spring

This gravel garden was relocated from one wall to another wall on April 20. Wheat grass, beans and pea shoots were planted. On August 8, the gravel garden was dismantled and relocated to a house in Maryland. The photos below show what grew from April to August 2015. The dismantling of the gravel bed is shown.

Beans   Wheatgrass

Beans   Wheatgrass

Beans   Wheatgrass

Pea Shoots

Gravel Relocation

Gravel Gardens on Cement - 2015 Summer

During the summer of 2015, the family moved to Ellicott City, MD, and the gravel garden was relocated. Gravel gardens on cement are ideal for portability so you don't have to loose the gravel quality accumulated over seasons of growth and decay and regrowth. This gravel has seen three seasons of growth, making it ideal to disassemble and relocate. In this garden pea shoots and beans were planted from seed, while mums and Hofstra were planted with soil balls from purchased potted plants. In August the mums were planted and flowered until October and then died out. The mum flowers came back in November. The Hofstra did not do well in gravel. The pea shoots grew three feet tall, flowered and grew pea pods.

August 21, 2015

August 21, 2015

August 28, 2015

Pea Shoots, Beans, Mums, Hofstra

September 4, 2015

Pea Shoots, Beans, Mums, Hofstra

October 3, 2015

November 7, 2015

Gravel Gardens on Cement - 2015 Summer

The soil ball of mums needed to acclimate to the gravel environment. The flowers died out and then return as shown below. On October 3, the flowers began coming back and by November 7, they had returned.

August 28, 2015

November 7, 2015

October 3, 2015

November 7, 2015

Gravel Gardens on Cement - 2016 Summer

Red spider mites joined the gravel growing ecosystem during the 2016 season, presumably being attracted by the cement surroundings. This hard-to-control infestation affected growth patterns and demonstrates that gravel cannot protect against spider mites.

May 20, 2016

Gravel Gardens on Cement - 2016 Summer

After one year, the family moved from an Ellicott City rental to the Ellicott City home. Below we see the disassembling of the gravel garden with the spider mites. The trash can helped relocate the gravel that we wanted to keep and relocate to the next house. The careful removal in transplanting of the growing plants enabled many of them to survive the transplanting process and the trip to the new home. Small bins provided ideal transplanting containers for the plants that grew by the move. A key aspect to gravel gardening is the portability benefit to relocate the gravel bed as needed while retaining matured gravel.

Above Ground Gravel Gardens - 2016 Summer

Once at the new location, the cinder blocks placed in a semicircle along a fence provided the barrier structure of the gravel garden. Since this particular gravel garden is constructed on grass, the normal risers needed to keep the gravel above the cement is not required. On grass, simply lay the plastic in the growing area then the lawn fabric on top of the plastic. Next, add sand on top of the lawn fabric and lay another layer of lawn fabric on top of the sand. Stack an additional layer of retaining brick walls and finally add 3 to 4 inches of gravel inside the retaining wall growing area. These gardens grew gladiolus beans and cucumbers as well as a jade plant in 2016, providing a second season for growing these crops.

June 2, 2016

June 2, 2016

June 2, 2016

June 25, 2016

Gladiolus

July 31, 2016

Beans and Cucumbers

August 9, 2016

Above Ground Gravel Gardens - 2016 Summer

The photos below taken on September 1 show cucumbers growing, picked and cut for dinner. Although cucumbers are reliable germinators in the gravel grow cups and can grow outdoors they often grow irregularly. It is possible that this above-ground gravel garden may retain less moisture than below-ground gravel gardens. The pickled cucumbers below grew into a tasty treat to kick off September along with a small crop. A key observation with growing cucumbers in Ellicott City, MD is that the deer will come and eat the cucumber flowers, which occurred during the growing season.

Above Ground Gravel Gardens - 2017 Summer

During the winter of early 2017 tulip bulbs placed in the above-ground gravel garden in January began to sprout by mid-April. Although by May 1 we witnessed the tulip blooms as well as the hyacinth bloom, each plant grew smaller in nature than typical tulips and hyacinths grown in soil. These micro hyacinths and micro tulips lasted for about two weeks and demonstrate a weakness with gravel gardens. The Asiatic lily below also grew meagerly compared to the Asiatic lily that grew in the indoor 16-ounce gravel grow cup. Growth outcome for some plants may be affected by the above- or below-ground nature of the outdoor gravel garden itself.

April 17, 2017

April 22, 2017

April 27, 2017

May 1, 2017

May 1, 2017

July 6, 2017

July 8, 2017

Gravel Gardening in Bags

Given the gravel moisture experiments with bags of gravel, we decided to look at gravel gardening right out of the bag. We cut a hole in the top of the bag to create the growing space. We punctured about 40 tiny holes on the bottom of the bag and placed the bag of gravel on a bag of sand. The bag of sand was cut in a similar fashion as the bag of gravel where the top part of the bag of sand was completely exposed. By placing the bag of gravel on the sand, the holes on the bottom of the gravel bag will allow moisture control and interface with the bag of sand beneath. The corn started off OK, but did not grow to full term, which shows that gravel can't do everything. The sunflower sprouts grew to full term, which is normally a few inches, but in this case, was left to grow to small tiny sunflower flowers. The peas did really well in the Quickrete gravel also found at Ace Hardware. The peas grew strong and hearty in the bag of gravel and were even on display at a trade show.

Corn — May 28, 2014	Corn — June 8, 2014
Sunflower Sprouts — May 28, 2014	Sunflower Sprouts — July 30, 2014
Peas — July 14, 2014	Peas — July 30, 2014

Gravel Gardening in Greenhouses

In greenhouse environments you will need to consider your own personal operation and how to adapt it using gravel and sand. You will also need to consider your transplanting or harvesting needs. By in large, you will place your seed in small containers and grow them to a certain height, usually under a foot for most items.

Configuration – In the container you select, you are simply putting an inch or two layer of sand and then gravel. Since the area is small and enclosed, water should spread evenly, and since weeds are not present, you don't need the fabric. The below photos depict examples of the depths to plant at in a small container and placing them in rows. You can also configure in tubs and other containers as shown in the transplant section. Be sure to plant in drainable containers. Below we have corn, beans and peas growing in gravel grow cups.

Watering – Depending on the temperature in the greenhouse, you could find yourself watering every three or four days if not daily. At home, I find myself watering a little more than outdoors. At home, this is the case because it's the winter and the house is at 65 to 80 degrees all day. Because the water can dry out faster, you want to keep the garden watered regularly. Fortunately, you only need a half cup of water or less. A spray can also do the trick.

Transplanting – With transplanting, you will need to determine your requirements. If you want to transplant your crops to soil, then we recommend carefully pouring out the gravel and sand, separating the seeding and transplant. You can reuse the gravel. Or you can empty the entire contents of the cup (sand, gravel and seedlings) into the transplant destination. Being all natural, sand, gravel and soil do well together.

Community Gravel Garden

This community gravel garden in Oakland, CA, depicts a few pea shoots growing in gravel. This garden was constructed in January 2015 with sprouts emerging two weeks later. A unique aspect of this gravel garden is that it hadn't rained in Oakland during the period as the city was undergoing a drought. Organizers did bring in a few buckets of water a few times to compensate.

The construction of this bed was slightly different where first the frame of the bed was made by laying bricks in a rectangle as shown in photo 1. In the same photo you see the 6 x 6 inch trench. Photo 2 depicts how plastic was placed in the bed with photo 3 showing the lawn fabric. Photo 4 shows the gravel garden at the end after the sand and gravel was put into the trench. After a few weeks, the pea shoot sprouts were up, looking promising.

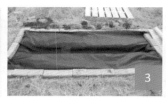

Gravel Gardening and Rooftops

"Green roofs" are nothing new. Society has experimented with elaborate and simple expressions of green roofs for decades. To date To Soil Less has not engaged in rooftop gardens but anticipates doing so in the near future. Gravel gardening is simply another item to consider in green roof design. The weight and space is comparable to existing formats of engineering. The difference with gravel green roofs is to insulate the roof in a manner that keeps the underbelly of the gravel garden cool.

On hot days the sun heats the roof and causes the underbelly of the garden to heat up, killing vegetation in the garden. The gravel garden is designed to repel heat from above, not below. A special foam layer is needed under the gravel to protect it from the hot roof.

Alternatives also include raising the entire bed off the roof, enclosing it in custom drainable insulated flower boxes or other creative ways to reduce the impact of heat related to the roof. There are 12 types of natural soil on the Earth, but there are thousands of types of sedimentary rock. All sedimentary rocks are different in composition. Consequently, testing is needed in every city independent of any other city.

In Washington, DC, of all the available gravel, Ace Hardware KolorScape brand has proven to be the best and most effective for growing crops. In every city, the best source of gravel for the specific climate of the city must be determined before consumer or commercial use.

Gravel Gardening and Rooftops

There are a variety of layers already embedded in the design of most green roofs.

As shown here from the www.grow-city.com and www.connaughtonconstruction.com websites, conventional rooftop garden diagrams display a layered set of materials with insulation, water proof membrane, etc.

With gravel gardens, a raised layer of sand about three inches deep and a layer of gravel about four inches deep replaces the current growing medium.

The key components of a well-designed rooftop gravel garden is properly tested gravel and properly insulating the bed from the heat of the roof.

Why are Gravel Gardens Good for Building Design?

✓Custom design for roofs, patios, decks and indoor lobby areas

✓Attractive to consumers and guests

✓Durable and practical

✓Once tested, you will plant what has been tested to do well in that gravel type

✓Custom low-cost irrigation integrated into the design

✓Low-cost materials such as river pea gravel are already a construction material often used

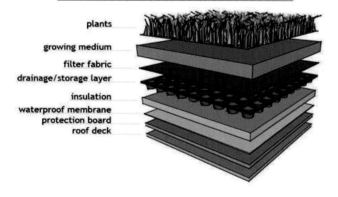

WHAT GOES INTO A 'GREEN ROOF'

- plants
- growing medium
- filter fabric
- drainage/storage layer
- insulation
- waterproof membrane
- protection board
- roof deck

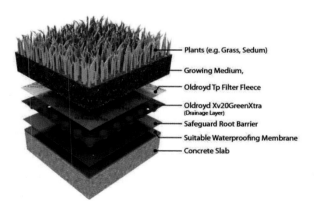

- Plants (e.g. Grass, Sedum)
- Growing Medium,
- Oldroyd Tp Filter Fleece
- Oldroyd Xv20GreenXtra (Drainage Layer)
- Safeguard Root Barrier
- Suitable Waterproofing Membrane
- Concrete Slab

Gravel Gardening and Small Farms

With row farms, you can water several ways. You can insert funnel pipes every 10 feet. When it rains, you will capture water, which will enable it to be stored and used for longer periods of time. If you have pre-existing irrigation equipment, you can place the water outlets near the sand. At the ends of the rows, you can have your water sources feed the end of the sand row on both sides. It will take 10 to 20 minutes depending on how long your planting rows are.

If you have long irrigation hoses, you can also place the hoses within the sand as well and supply water via your hosing system. You will need to keep your tractor row mowed so that you can walk through the farming area and reduce the chances of weed spores floating into the gravel. This method will reduce the chances of you having to weed as much. Also be careful when harvesting with a tractor as the rocks can get kicked up into the tractor equipment inner workings.

Although gravel applications can be good for commercial farms, the national supply of gravel is not yet suited for a widespread use of gravel in agriculture by large farmers. Home and community garden demand is suitable to current river gravel supply. Large farms are not. Large farms should only do this on a limited basis and only in states that have large gravel supplies that will not disrupt environmental necessities.

As previously mentioned, all applications of commercial gravel activity should be tested on a limited basis in year one for the specific type of crop being planted. Retrofitting an acre of land into gravel rows is estimated to cost about $50,000 an acre or more. So you want to be sure the crop you seek to grow does exactly what you want it to do in gravel and completes a full lifecycle before investing large amounts to retrofit your land.

String Beans

Gravel Gardening and Small Farms

Large-scale farming with gravel can be accomplished with gravel rows. The depth of the gravel row will depend on what you want to grow. As with most farming, try to farm on land that is flat, although slightly sloped land is OK as well. With gravel rows, you want to space lines three feet apart where you have a three-foot planting row and a three-foot tractor or walking row. This if is you want to harvest using a tractor or manually.

Next you have to dig the necessary trench along the center of the planting row. If you do this process manually, then keep the lines down. If you use a tractor with the necessary attachment you will need to remove the lines so the lines don't get entangled in the tractor. Dig the trench to be about 10 to 12 inches deep. This is done to help minimize watering where a good rain could keep it watered longer. Also, the depth is ideal for natural durability of the system. You also want to dig the planting row down about four inches as well. This will make is so that you don't have to necessarily include a retaining wall. You can have a retaining wall if you want, especially for in-ground crops that require more of an air-tight system.

When laying the fabric, crop fruit development is important. For crops that fruit above ground, you can lay the industrial and then the capillary fabric and keep the depth at 3 to 4 inches. For crops that grow below ground and you need a deeper depth of approximately 10 inches, then you need to lay plastic first followed by the industrial and finally the capillary material. With in-ground fruiting crops, your initial trench should be 12 inches below the 10-inch trench. See the diagram below and photos on the next page.

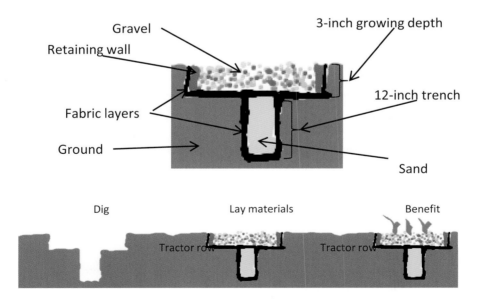

159

Gravel Gardening and Small Farms

The first step is to flatten an area and dig a trench as shown in photo A. The trench was dug with a back hoe and the sides are being flattened by a bull dozer. Next lay plastic as shown in photo B. Be sure to fasten in the ground along the trench. Photo C depicts laying the layer of black fabric. Because the plastic was thick, we did not have a layer of industrial fabric. Photo D shows where sand was placed in the trench and photo E shows the sand after it was covered with fabric. Gravel is being poured in photos F and G. The 125 x 12 foot field gravel garden is completed in photo H. See the before and after photos on the following page.

Gravel Gardening and Small Farms

Beans and corn planted July 1

Photo taken August 18 after 40 days of 100+ degrees and no manual watering

We harvested beans by surprise on October 18 with no manual watering during the low-rain period. The corn did not make it in these conditions.

Beans were picked on October 18; they could have been picked earlier but the field was not being regularly monitored.

Survival Gravel Gardens

Going soil-less with gravel gardening can have global implications as for the first time, one can go to the beach or river in a forest and make a sustainable vegetable-producing garden with nothing but the shirt on your back.

Survival gravel garden steps at a beach or forest river include the following:

1. As you have already learned, the primary ingredients for gravel gardens are sand, rocks from water, and capillary material.

2. With your shirt serving as the capillary material, one can take sand and gravel from the beach or river bed and create a gravel garden. The nature of the beach or river will determine how long you have to search for rocks.

3. Once you gather your rocks and or shells from the ocean or river, be sure to break the rocks into small gravel-size pieces. Use a big rock to break smaller rocks and shells into gravel-size pieces as shown in this manual.

4. Locate a space away from the beach, clear an area, dig the trench and lay leaves first to serve as the plastic-like layer barrier to separate the sand underneath with the gravel garden.

5. Place your t-shirt over the leaves in the trench and surrounding area. You should cut your shirt so that you can use both the front and back for a larger growing area.

6. Next, pour the sand in the trench. You can put leaves over the visible sand so that the gravel is poured on the leaves and shirt. The leaves will naturally allow water to soak through to the gravel.

7.   Identify available items for the border: large stones, wood, sticks, etc. Place a border around the gravel garden.

8.   Finally, lay the gravel or rocks that you gathered from the ocean or river bed. Try to have a minimum of two inches of gravel.

9.   Ocean water will kill the gravel garden. On a deserted island, you will need to accumulate water via the morning dew and occasional rains.

The only thing missing is seed, so you will need to bring or find your own. This application using beach materials allows coastal countries to grow crops and vegetation without the need for soil and fertilizers.   Survival packs of the future will have seeds like pea shoots and beans that seem to grow well in most river pea gravel types.

The images below depict micro greens and peas growing in gravel that was obtained from the Chesapeake Bay, crushed with a hammer and set up in a gravel grow cup. After two weeks, both seed types did well, illustrating that the coast can now cultivate crops.

June 8, 2014

June 8, 2014

Micro Greens   Peas

June 22, 2014

June 22, 2014

Survival Gravel Gardens – Myrtle Beach, SC

While at Myrtle Beach, SC, I went searching for rocks along the beach but only found crushed sea shells. Recognizing that sea shell are also sedimentary, I decided to experiment with a few sunflower micro greens and alfalfa sprouts. It did not take long for the germination to occur and within a week, we had good emergence as shown in the photos below.

It is likely that sea shells actually add more organic and nutritional value to the seeds than gravel since the sea shells are likely much younger in sedimentary aspects than their rock counterpart. The rocks formed over thousands of years, but life existed in the sea shells likely within the past decade or so, making them rich with organic materials.

Therefore, if stranded on a deserted island or in the wilderness, should your survival kit have micro greens and sprout seeds, you may just be able to survive if you can find a river, lake, stream or ocean for its sedimentary materials.

Alfalfa Sprouts

June 11, 2014

Sunflower Micro Greens

June 19, 2014

Alfalfa Sprouts

June 24, 2014

Sunflower Micro Greens   Alfalfa Sprouts

June 24, 2014

Survival Gravel Gardens - Corn

During the 2015 trip to Myrtle Beach, gathered shells were placed in a re-sealable plastic bag with sand at the bottom. Corn seeds were placed in the shells on a Monday and by Friday the corn sprouts below emerged.

Survival Gravel Gardens – Outer Banks, NC

During the annual summer trip in 2016, the family picked the Outer Banks, NC as the summer destination. The rocks from the shores of North Carolina were smaller in size than the rocks from Ace Hardware. True to form, the fresh sedimentary beach rock grew bean mix, sunflower sprouts and wheatgrass within one week in the recycled grave grow cup.

July 1, 2016

July 6, 2016

Bean Mix, Sunflower and Wheatgrass

July 2, 2016

Sunflower Micro Greens

July 3, 2016

Sunflower Micro Greens

July 6, 2016

Bean Mix Sprouts

Survival Gravel Gardens – Miami Beach, FL

During a business trip to South Beach Miami, a few rocks found at sea were picked up. The South Beach sea rocks, broken with a hammer and configured into a gravel grow cup with marijuana seeds and wheatgrass seeds, grew both plants within one week. Consistent with other fresh sedimentary rock, growth rates tend to be faster with beach sedimentary rock than when growing with store-bought sedimentary rock.

May 19, 2017

Marijuana

Wheatgrass

May 26, 2017

May 29, 2017

Survival Gravel Gardens – Patuxent River

Behind the Ellicott City, MD, home is a river that leads into the Patuxent River. Rocks gathered from the river and crushed with a hammer were used in a gravel grow cup experiment. Pea shoots and wheatgrass grew at their normal rate in the Patuxent River rock. This experiment represented the first river rock experiment of this nature where those lost in the woods could replicate this and develop gardens for quick nutrition access.

Pea shoots

Pea shoots

Wheatgrass

Pea shoots

Wheatgrass

Survival Gravel Gardens – Martha's Vineyard

In 2017 the family went to Martha's Vineyard. While there, rock from the famous Inkwell served as the growing medium for pea shoots and cucumbers in the gravel grow cup assembled on August 13. Sand was not present during assembly. A napkin served as a substitute to the sand, which is why the image on August 13 has white at the bottom. A t-shirt, napkin, paper, towel or other cotton fabric can serve as a substitute to sand if sand is not available. The purpose of the sand is to absorb water and distribute it to the gravel as naturally necessary. Any number of substances can absorb water, from those items already listed to a sponge, wash cloth, cotton balls, etc. In all likelihood, however, since sand is sedimentary and all-natural, it is likely the most ideal for root development. Conversely, sand can decay. It is also possible that the rate of decay in napkins or cotton balls may be lower.

In any event, when stranded on a deserted island or in the wilderness, should your survival kit have micro greens and sprout seeds, you may just be able to survive if you can find a river, lake, stream or ocean for its sedimentary materials.

August 13, 2017

Pea Shoots and Cucumbers

August 19, 2017

Pea Shoots and Cucumbers

August 26, 2017

Chapter 3 Summary

The outdoor chapter of gravel gardening provided the materials, assembly steps and methodologies necessary to construct an outdoor gravel growing ecosystem in a variety of settings. Outside there are several key takeaways when gardening with gravel:

In ground gravel Gardens. The in-ground gravel garden is the most ideal setup for outdoor gardens. This configuration, assemble properly, allows the greatest degree of moisture retention in the ecosystem. Three to four inches of gravel is ideal but users may assemble a gravel Garden that has up to 6 or 7 inches deep of gravel.

Above-ground gravel gardens. The above-ground garden will grow many types of crops successfully. A minor limitation of these gardens is moisture control and weather vulnerability. Users me account for this by lining the walls of the gravel garden with additional layers of plastic and lawn fabric for added insulation.

Outdoor gardening benefits: The amount of benefits for outdoor growing are numerous with key benefits highlighted below.

> **Water conservation** – The sand water retention reservoir maintains moisture and minimizes manual watering needs.
> **Sustainable** – The low cost nature, lack of nutrients and soil, and global availability of sedimentary rock suggests that gravel gardening is likely the most organic and sustainable growing method to exist.
> **Outdoor organics** – The bugs, bees and suns that beams, benefit the blooms and buds of the bulbs that breed. Outdoor life tends to enhance the outcome of plants grown in gravel, making outdoor gardens more productive than indoor gravel gardens.
> **Durability.** A properly assembled outdoor gravel Garden will grow plants for several decades. Each year the gravel ages in organic viability so that the organic value of the gravel bed improves annually.

Gardening on cement surfaces. On cement the gravel grown ecosystem should be raised above the cement so that the Heat on a hot day doesn't cook the gravel garden From Below. This objective can be raised either by assembling an outdoor Garden on a table or on risers.

Survival gravel gardens. Rock's found along coastlines and in rivers in forest areas are capable of sustaining plant life when properly assembled.

Chapter 4
Outdoor Observations

Gravel Garden Ecosystem

The ecosystem of the gravel growing environment is inclusive of the organic cycle between the roots, gravel, water, sand and other organic materials such as leaves and pollen. Generally speaking, the ecosystem is constantly expanding as long as moisture impacts the gravel, affecting root expansion. Closed ecosystems like those with gravel grow cups accumulate decay faster than an open gravel ecosystem found outdoors.

The ecosystem of the gravel garden appears to be generally strong and healthy, as a variety of outdoor bugs sometime find a habitat in the nutrient-rich environment. To test your ecosystem, after a few days of using your gravel garden, when you water the bed for a few minutes, worms should rise to the top of the garden. This suggests that the worms are in the system, consuming organic matter and secreting soil. This accumulating process in the ecosystem helps maintain a healthy growing environment for plants.

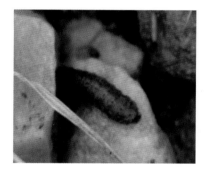

Adjacent the rocks where the grass is growing is a little bug hanging out. Worms, slugs, ants, spiders and all types of bugs seem to enjoy the river-based rock. We do say that this approach is similar to the coral reef where thousands of species live. In this growing environment, the presence of life forms suggests a strong ecological construct suitable for vegetation development.

The broccoli never had a chance with these broccoli worms. As soon as the broccoli grew the worms were on them all summer. This broccoli was planted with the cucumbers in 2011. Broccoli worms chew irregular holes in the leaves and usually eat their way into broccoli heads from the bottom. We are not sure where they came from but they were not there before the broccoli and disappeared after the broccoli was eaten. Unfortunately, gravel cannot prevent Mother Nature's presence of other animal life that can eat plants and vegetation.

Although it is a fairly disgusting sight, this slug is perched on the gravel. The slug's presence is another testimony to the ecological environment provided by the gravel and vegetation.

Water and Gravel

Hydrology is the scientific study of the properties, distribution and effects of water on the Earth's surface, in the soil and underlying rocks, and in the atmosphere, according to www.dictionary.com.

Hydrology by definition has several aspects that are inherent in gravel gardening: 1) having water or moisture within the ground on the Earth's surface keeps the sand area cool so that water does not evaporate; 2) retarding water from getting into the atmosphere by holding water in the sand; and 3) interfacing with moisture in the air during the photosynthesis process.

Gravel and sand creates a hydrological system where water is conserved by storing the water in the sand, allowing water to be dispersed slowly via capillary actions to the surface. In soil, water escapes faster, especially during droughts, which causes the surface of the ground to crack, letting water evaporate into the atmosphere. The gravel goes a step further and prevents water evaporation, thus making more of it available for the plants' metabolism and dedicated for root growth.

Generally speaking, you should water once every seven days if outdoors and once every three or four days indoors. When outdoors, the Earth keeps the water cool. The layers of fabric retain the water, so moisture can be consistent. Indoors, the Earth is not providing the insulation, so room temperature can affect evaporation to a greater degree. Planting in pots can also have similar water issues. To compensate, simply create an enclosed sand and gravel growing environment. This is easily done by lining the pot with plastic.

With gravel the water hydrology allows for a sustained presence of water. The sun typically reflects off of the rock so that only ½ inch of the top of the gravel bed is affected by the sun. Underneath the ½ inch it remains moist for days and sometimes weeks without additional watering. The gravel system allows water to be retained in a sustained fashion.

Gravel Moisture

The cup shown below was not watered. It was assembled and left under a heat vent by accident. As you can see, beads of moisture have built up on the inside of the cup. One of the great properties of rocks is that they sweat in heat, drawing moisture out of the air. The moisture is enough to activate the chemical action to begin the geological agricultural process. If you look closely, you will notice that the sunflower sprouts planted have already begun to germinate.

The Campbell Equation of Water + River Rock = Plant Food hinges on water. With rock being able to sweat, water is created and is referred to as "gravel moisture." The amount of water created is unknown. To best illustrate the effects of gravel moisture, take a bag of gravel that was bought at a hardware store. The bag is usually clear plastic with no graphic on the back on the bag so that you can see the gravel. If you place the bag in the sun on a hot day, you will notice that after a few hours, condensation has started and beads of water will accumulate inside the bag of gravel on the plastic. The bag creates a sauna effect where moisture is being created through the bag. In the cup below, the heat activated the natural sauna enough to initiate germination.

The amount of water accumulated per square inch at varying temperatures will be the foundation of academic and scientific study. We see that rocks naturally have a moisture creation effect, enabling gravel gardens to support certain types of plant life in drought conditions. Simple experiments have been conducted by the Peace Corps Volunteer program where they extract water from the air and capture it using simple materials. It is likely that simple materials can be assembled to capture and measure moisture growth rates in gravel gardening as well.

Heat and Gravel

A

Drought-Like Conditions – At the start of a drought period in early July 2012, To Soil Less established a large gravel garden in the middle of open land, planted a few rows of bean and corn seeds but did not water nor fertilize. We wanted to figure out what would happen if you did nothing; no watering, no fertilizer, just open 100+ degree sun. By mid-August, both the corn and beans had grown about 6 to 10 inches (see photo C) and by mid-October a small crop of beans was harvested (see photos D).

B

Observations reveal that when the initial gravel field was installed, planted rows were dug with a shovel as shown in photo A. Photo B, on the other hand, depicts what was happening just 1.5 inches beneath the surface. A "condensation effect" between the rock cooking at 100+ degrees on the outside and the Earth cooling the base of the enclosed gravel structure a few inches below on the inside created moisture.

C

Additional experiments found that when you have 100+ degrees on the outside of the gravel, it can be as cool as 75 degrees a few inches below the surface. The stark difference in temperature results in condensation or moisture being created with the gravel. Given the results of the corn and beans in photos C and D, it appears that the moisture was enough to sustain plant life for the beans at least.

D

Further tests are required in a variety of high temperature outdoor environments. The theory that condensation is created naturally absent of a water source can have positive outcomes for gravel gardens in hot climates.

Gravel and Bees

Bees seem to adapt well to gravel-grown plants. These images of the cantaloupe plant, sunflower, and squash are of bees interfacing with the pollen of the plant. The pollen in the squash plant seems so rich that the bees appeared to be somewhat intoxicated and semi-dormant as they curl around the core of a flower. Additional research is needed to determine if gravel grown plants aid in the sustainment of bee populations.

Cantaloupe

Squash

Sunflower

Gravel and Disease

Squash

Squash

When it comes to plant diseases gravel can limit or minimize the availability and presence of inground diseases or diseases that occur due to soil contamination. Airborne diseases however will still adversely affect plant growth in gravel. The leaves on this page of plants growing and gravel demonstrate that adverse airborne contaminants, diseases, and bugs will eat and degrade plants. Consequently gravel only minimizes plant disease of roots but the leaves are fully exposed to airborne diseases in the atmosphere.

Zinnia

Summer Squash

The affected leaves shown of the squash at the top are the leaves at the bottom of the squash plant while the actual squash is ready for harvest. Even though the leaf is decaying, the plant is still producing. Conversely, the zinnia leaf disease significantly limited the zinnia bloom of this particular plant. Also, the summer squash at the bottom right corner never made it as its leaves ended up dying before the plant could grow.

Root Behavior - Containers

The roots inside pots, grow cups and other containers tend to bore down into the sand, turning to run parallel with the sand in layers as depicted below. The roots also grow into the sand, but over time the bottom inch of gravel becomes a complex matrix of intertwining roots systems from various plants totally consuming the sand. The takeaway is that gravel roots layer themselves at the point with the most moisture and nutrients – between the sand and the gravel. Roots tend to absorb food from the gravel and moisture from the sand.

Corn Root Behavior and Gravel

These corn roots were taken up at the Lowell School gravel garden at the end of the season. As you can see, the roots wrap themselves around the rocks, which helps sustain the root system.

When taking up plants and roots at the end of the season, it is good to shake out the gravel so that you not only retain the gravel in the bed, but you also benefit from the decay that these specific rocks have with the root systems. The rocks that are in closer proximity to direct contact with roots will likely develop layers of organic decay on the rocks in subsequent years. These rocks or enriched gravel appreciate in organic material, enabling the gravel bed to strengthen each year. Fallen leaves also support gravel appreciation, but direct contact creates a better ecosystem of enriched gravel.

Scallions Root Behavior and Gravel

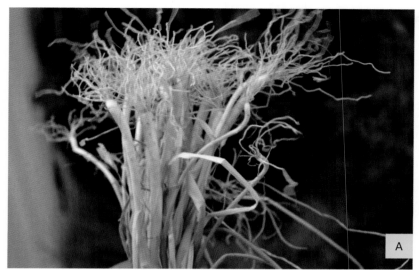

These scallion roots look just like the ones sold in grocery stores. The roots appear healthy with good color. Photo A was taken in mid-June while photos B and D were taken in mid-July.

As shown, the roots only extend a few inches and come out fairly clean as the rocks did not embed themselves among the roots.

Grass Root Behavior and Gravel

Earlier in this book information was provided about grass that was planted late in March 2011. This photo was taken in February 2012. The interesting thing about this experiment is that the grass is still visible and green. The roots did not freeze and die like the other plants. Also, these seeds were planted in larger rocks, also from the river. We don't advise growing your grass in gravel because cutting becomes an issue. The rocks would kick up in the blades of a mower and cause damage. We planted grass to test the gravel effect on grass seeds.

As you get closer on the gravel you will see how the base of the grass blade comes out of the gravel. You also see a small slug hanging out on the gravel. As a point of reference, when I planted this grass seed in gravel, I also planted grass seed in my yard. The gravel-grown grass grew quicker and thicker.

The roots of the grass on the left photo seem to intertwine together into the sand, which could explain the cold resiliency. You can see new grass blades coming out of the side on the left photo. Unseasonably warm winters can cause bulbs to sprout early like these grass blades. If you look closer, you can see the rocks again embedded within the root system.

Mums Root Behavior – From Soil to Gravel

These mums were planted in this raised gravel bed in late August. They died after a month like the ones in the pot but came back as shown in mid-November. In December, we had to relocate the raised gravel bed and noticed the roots of the mums had grown into the gravel from the soil. You will notice in photos 4 and 5 that the roots have even wrapped themselves around the gravel, growing about six inches into the gravel. Photo 6 shows that even after relocating and transplanting the potted mums, the mums are still flowering in December, nearly four months later.

1
August 28, 2014

2
November 11, 2014

3
December 10, 2014

4
December 10, 2014

5
December 10, 2014

6
December 24, 2014

Chapter 5
Academic Studies

GWU – Gravel Composting Study

Gravel composting is the process that happens naturally with gravel gardening where at the end of the season, the remaining vines, leaves and leftover vegetation decay and decompose back into the gravel garden. The theory of gravel composting suggests that the gravel beds appreciate in impact each successive year. During the annual ecological cycle, the gravel garden goes though a variety of composting-related activities, including worms that find refuge in gravel, the secretions of roots systems, and the pollen and leaves that decay and wash away into the gravel bed. All of these elements appear to add organic substance to gravel beds each year.

George Washington University professor Dr. H. Henry Teng of the Department of Chemistry & Environmental Resource Policy Program in Washington, DC, sough to examine the notion of accumulated organic matter on gravel used for growing crops versus fresh gravel. He was provided gravel samples that had produced crops for 20 years and a sample of gravel that had not been used for crop cultivation. Under a high intensity microscope, Dr. Teng crushed the two samples to dust fragments and then examined the gravel at 7,400 times magnification. Upon comparison at this magnification, Dr. Teng noticed a distinct layer of rigid material on the 20-year-old gravel surface that was not on the fresh gravel. The images below depict the rigidness of the 20-year-old gravel surface against fresh gravel at 7,400 times magnification.

Element Number	Element Symbol	Element Name	Confidence	Concentration	Error
14	Si	Silicon	100.0	24.3	1.9
8	O	Oxygen	100.0	72.0	2.2
6	C	Carbon	Manual	3.7	6.0

The fresh gravel elemental composition is listed above, which depicts normal ranges of silicon, oxygen and carbon.

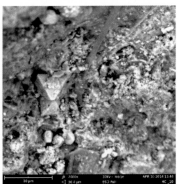

Element Number	Element Symbol	Element Name	Confidence	Concentration	Error
8	O	Oxygen	100.0	58.7	2.1
14	Si	Silicon	100.0	10.2	2.4
6	C	Carbon	Manual	2.5	4.5
7	N	Nitrogen	Manual	7.9	5.0
20	Ca	Calcium	Manual	4.7	5.1
13	Al	Aluminum	Manual	1.9	7.6
26	Fe	Iron	Manual	11.4	8.1
15	P	Phosphorus	Manual	1.2	10.8
12	Mg	Magnesium	Manual	1.5	11.8

The 20-year-old gravel's elemental composition is listed above, which depicts a host of elements in varying composite percentages. These materials are basic trace organic elements that have accumulated on the surface of the gravel. The additional elements support the notion that gravel garden rocks accumulate organic material over time.

The image to the right is magnified 7,400 times and depicts what appears to be root residue on a gravel fragment that has been used for crops cultivation for only three years. The pattern of the root residue suggests that the roots are attaching to the rocks for the apparent nutrients contained in the rocks.

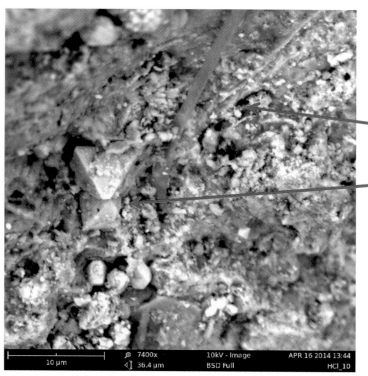

In this version on the 20-year-old gravel, root residue fragments are also apparent.

Another key item to point out is the pyramid-shaped formation on the gravel. This suggests geological crystallization, which occurs during the sediment development process.

Element Number	Element Symbol	Element Name	Confidence	Concentration	Error
14	Si	Silicon	100.0	22.8	0.9
8	O	Oxygen	100.0	63.7	1.0
6	C	Carbon	Manual	2.1	3.8
26	Fe	Iron	Manual	7.9	6.9
13	Al	Aluminium	Manual	0.9	9.3
11	Na	Sodium	Manual	1.5	13.0
12	Mg	Magnesium	Manual	0.9	12.4

The top image is a close up of the image on the lower right side. The lower image is a 7,400-time magnification of the 20-year-old gravel depicting the rough exterior surface from years of decay (rights side) against the inside of the same piece of gravel fragment (left side). The average composition chart pertains to composition inside the 20-year-old gravel. On the prior page, we provided the composition of the exterior of the 20-year-old gravel. Above on this page, the average core composition of the gravel is listed. As you can see, the core has less "other" elements than the exterior.

You may also recall that the average composition of fresh gravel was more simple that what is listed here. It is not yet clear why the interior of the 20-year-old gravel would have these levels of "other" materials while the fresh gravel did not.

GWU – Gravel Composting Study

Key findings by Dr. Teng in conducting preliminary tests on gravel used for crop cultivation include the following:

1) **Gravel Composting** – Gravel that undergoes a cycle of growing crops will likely leave organic material in the gravel garden growing environment. The organic materials found on 20-year-old gravel was composed of nitrogen, calcium, aluminum, iron, phosphorus and magnesium, all of which make up the components of an accumulated soil-like layer of organic matter building slowly on the exterior of the gravel. Given the nature of gravel, it is likely that composting naturally occurs with gravel gardens.

2) **Gravel Variability** – In examining two types of gravel sold in standard packaging, it is apparent that both types of gravel have 4 to 8 different types of rocks within the gravel. In the brown Tennessee gravel this is less apparent because of a brownish coat over the gravel. But once you look closely and wash away the top layer of dust you find about six slightly different rock types and small sea shells. The Ace Hardware KolorScape gravel, which is beige in color, has about 7 or 8 different rock types depending on how you classify the differences. The key notion is to recognize the variability. The key is to determine which rock does what with respect to plant growth and development. See images below.

3) **Root Presence** – It is obvious that roots are digging into the gravel in what appears to be specific root growth formation and patterns. Root residue was found on both gravel samples that produced crops. The root patterns were consistent with root growth when seeking and finding nutrients. Given the microscopic nature of the images, this suggests that the roots may fully wrap around a piece of gravel in its development.

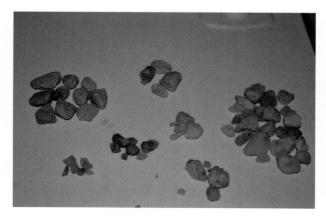

Old Castle KolorScape Pea Gravel

Tennessee Brown River Gravel

Gravel, Oxygen, Energy and Decay

Wikipedia tells us that in chemistry, chemical energy is the potential of a chemical substance to undergo a transformation through a chemical reaction or to transform other chemical substances. Breaking or making of chemical bonds involves energy, which may be either absorbed or evolved from a chemical system. Energy that can be released (or absorbed) because of a reaction between a set of chemical substances is equal to the difference between the energy content of the products and the reactants. Consequently, chemical energy is generated between the gravel, water, seeds and roots.

Newtonian mechanics shares that between two or more masses (or other forms of energy–momentum) a gravitational potential energy exists. Within gravel gardens, in general, gravitational energy is at play. However, within the gravel grow cup, the build-up in chemical and gravitational energy can sour at times without oxygen. Because of this, tiny holes are recommended to oxygenate the growing environment. Without the holes, some seed types can decay and decompose in low oxygen gravel grow cups as shown in the images. Should this type of decay arise, simply puncture a few tiny holes and the oxygen will eventually clear up the decay as it decomposes back into the gravel.

In the gravel grow cup, accumulating chemical and gravitational energy creates an expanding ecosystem when adding growing roots from multiple seeds. The result can be a petri dish of activity until such time that everything dies completely. Eventually, the sediment of the decay will absorb into the gravel. Users should be mindful of the energy build-up in gravel grow cups.

The decay itself is actually good for the ecosystem overall. The black build-up on the sides represents the building blocks of the creation of soil, while the green decay represents the build-up of algae. Both elements are good for adding organic material to the gravel ecosystem as explained by Dr. Teng of George Washington University.

189

TSU Germination Study

Dr. Arvazena (Zena) Clardy, an assistant professor of Horticulture, 4-H SET and NRCS Outreach at the College of Agriculture, Human and Natural Sciences at Tennessee State University conducted a germination study with her Plant Science and Floriculture class. Dr. Clardy looked at simple germination in cups using Tennessee brown river gravel against 39 different seed types. The basic findings of the study are below.

1. **Germination** - Of the 39 experiments conducted, 34 germinated and 29 had emergence and grew to a transplantable state. All of the seeds that were germinated and the seedlings that emerged had good green color and appeared healthy. Shoot and root systems were well developed with some growing several inches in gravel during the 30-day observation period.

2. **Transplanting** – Most seeds germinated, seedlings demonstrated good emergence and appeared ready for transplanting as the roots and shoots seemed very healthy and strong.

3. **Gravel Depths in Cups** - More shallow depths of gravel tend to do better than deeper depths. There appears to be an optimal depth for germination and emergence in cups, which is about halfway in the gravel. There is a specific growing range within the gravel environment where the seeds must germinate and grow properly. If the seeds fall below that range, then the shoots may likely not reach the surface before dying out. If the seeds are too close to the top, they will likely not receive the necessary moisture and water to leach nutrients from the gravel. Generally, the seed located in the center of the two-inch range will likely have the best chance of being moist and close enough to the top so that emergence is easier to achieve. In the taller cup, seed germination occurred consistently as with the shorter cups, but shoot development was much less pronounced. In the taller cups, the shoots of most of the seeds in the study grew slower than the shoots in the shorter cups. In the taller cups, the shoots have longer to travel to get to the surface while in the shorter cups the shoots reach the top quicker and develop faster.

TSU student Angela Washington growing basil – photo taken in week 3.

TSU student Amber Lee growing carnations – photo taken in week 4.

4. **Seed Size** - Small tiny seeds should be poured on the top as they can fall to the bottom and not reach the top. This was the case with several small seed types that germinated but did not emerge to the top of the gravel. This was especially in the taller cups, where it was visible that tiny seeds that germinated made attempts to climb up through the rocks, but could not and ultimately died.

5. **Seed Knowledge** – It is important to read the normal directions of the seeds being planted; some seeds have longer germinating periods than others. So, it is good to set a margin of expectation based on what is already known about the plant variety. Also, some plants do better in the spring, when it may be a little cooler, while others may do better in the hot summer or fall. (Cool season and Warm season varieties)

6. **Watering Schedule** – Watering in gravel is not the same as watering in soil. With gravel it is best to water indoors when the drip cup basin is dry, which should be every 6 to 8 days. Then water once and refill. The natural effects of the sand seem to help maintain moisture in the gravel system so that the wet gravel can leach nutrients for the plant root systems. Some soil-based seeds recommend watering every few days.

7. **Gravel Comparison** – One student compared gravel to outside soil and potting mix. The results showed that gravel grew the five test seeds better than outside soil, but slightly less than the potting mix. Where seed x may have grown five inches in gravel, it grew 5.5 inches in potting mix. Although gravel appears to be less impactful than the potting mix, the potting mix has been scientifically enhanced to produce crops.

TSU student Jennifer Williams growing spinach – photo taken in week 2.

TSU student Caroline Huffines growing broccoli – photo taken in week 3.

TSU student collection of experiments – photo taken 3 weeks after seeding.

TSU Germination Study

The chart below lists the various experiments conducted by TSU students in Dr. Clardy's Plant Science and Floriculture class. The chart lists the number of total experiments, the number of seeds that germinated and that grew to a transplantable state, the number of seeds that germinated, the number that emerged, the relative state of the root system and the basic ability to transplant. The results are sorted by those that were not able to grow to a transplantable state first, followed by those that germinated, emerged and grew to a transplantable state. The results of this test depicts what germinates. To answer the question of what grows best, it is always going to be dependent on your gravel type, seed type and climate.

# Experiments	# Germination to transplant	Seed Type	Germination	Emergence	Root Systems	Ability to Transplant
1		Lavender	Yes	Yes	Weak	No
2		Lavender - 2	Yes	Yes	Weak	No
3		Lettuce	No	No	No	No
4		Lima Beans	No	no	No	No
5		Moss Rose	Yes	No	No	No
6		Moss Rose - 2	No	No	No	No
7		Oregano	Yes	No	No	No
8		Oregano - 2	Yes	No	No	No
9		Rosemary	No	No	No	No
10		Viola Tricolor	No	No	No	No
11	1	Alyssum	Yes	Yes	Developed	Yes
12	2	Basil	Yes	Yes	Developed	Yes
13	3	Broccoli	Yes	Yes	Developed	Yes
14	4	Broccoli 2	Yes	Yes	Developed	Yes
15	5	Carnation	Yes	Yes	Developed	Yes
16	6	Carrots	Yes	Yes	Developed	Yes
17	7	Carrots - 2	Yes	Yes	Developed	Yes
18	8	Carrots - 3	Yes	Yes	Developed	Yes
19	9	Chives	Yes	Yes	Developed	Yes
20	10	Chives - 2	Yes	Yes	Developed	Yes
21	11	Chives - 3	Yes	Yes	Developed	Yes
22	12	Cucumbers	Yes	Yes	Developed	Yes
23	13	Garden Beans	Yes	Yes	Developed	Yes
24	14	Greens	Yes	Yes	Developed	Yes
25	15	Hot Peppers	Yes	Yes	Developed	Yes
26	16	Marigolds	Yes	Yes	Developed	Yes
27	17	Onion	Yes	Yes	Developed	Yes
28	18	Onion - 2	Yes	Yes	Developed	Yes
29	19	Parsley	Yes	Yes	Developed	Yes
30	20	Parsley - 2	Yes	Yes	Developed	Yes
31	21	Peppers - 2	Yes	Yes	Developed	Yes
32	22	Pumpkins	Yes	Yes	Developed	Yes
33	23	Pumpkins - 2	Yes	Yes	Developed	Yes
34	24	Spinach	Yes	Yes	Developed	Yes
35	25	Spinach - 2	Yes	Yes	Developed	Yes
36	26	Squash	Yes	Yes	Developed	Yes
37	27	Tomatoes	Yes	Yes	Developed	Yes
38	28	Watermelon	Yes	Yes	Developed	Yes
39	29	Yellow Flowers	Yes	Yes	Developed	Yes

Chapter 6
Living With Your Gravel Garden

Living With Your Gravel Garden

Now that you have a better understanding of the gravel growing method, let us re-examine the advantages to your new gravel garden:

1. **Weeds** – Since we have two layers of fabric underlining the garden bed, in-ground weeds do not grow. You will still have airborne weeds, but because of the gravel, they pull up easily. When pulling any airborne weeds, you can leave the weeds on the gravel and it will decay and add nutrients to the gravel bed.

2. **The Trench** – Feel free to dig a deeper trench. The basic outcome is a larger sand storage space. You can also add organic matter to your trench to serve as natural fertilizers.

3. **Fallen Vegetation** – Leaves, sticks and other airborne vegetation will fall on your gravel garden. Allow them to decay into the garden. These natural elements end up providing natural fertilizers in the growing environment. Their presence adds to nitrogen fixation to assist in plant growth.

4. **Time** – Over time, fallen vegetation, dried root systems (over the winter) and other natural microorganisms will strengthen the subsequent years' growing environments. Each season, the vegetation will compost and re-compost back into the gravel. This should assist with better nitrogen fixation in future years.

5. **Watering** – You really only need to water the outdoor garden once every 7 to 10 days, but feel free to water more if you want. If you would like to water more and/or use fertilizer, you can expect to have faster growth rates.

6. **Insects and Such** – With gravel, you will have less insects in your garden area than with soil. But in nature, there will always be life crawling about. Fencing, netting or doming an area can also prevent passage of insects and such. Some vegetation naturally attracts insects, so additional natural remedies are available depending on the crop.

7. **Funnel Pipe** – You can attach any type of funnel system to the pipe. Naturally, having a larger bucket is better as it can hold more water. You can also have a wider PVC pipe. Both of these additions will increase the amount of time that overflow water is allowed to saturate the system. This extends the time that water will impact the system and increases the level of moisture in the growing environment. This aspect generally can lead to a faster growth rate in the plants. The bucket can also act as a rain catch basin. To take advantage of this feature, simply put a layer of cotton (jean-thick material) at the top of the pipe in the bottom of the bucket. The layer of material will allow rain water to store and will permeate through to the sand over time.

8. **Fertilizers** – Although you do not need fertilizers nor do we encourage the use of fertilizers, one can still add fertilizer and it will undoubtedly increase production.

9. **Maintenance** – Generally speaking, you should not have to ever change the gravel bed. The rocks will last 100 years and the fabric 20. You will need to weed airborne weeds, but actually in this case, those weeds can add nutrients to the growing environment. Therefore, weed as necessary, but leave the pulled weeds to decompose.

10. **Seeding** – In the beginning, seed liberally to see how they do. As you can see in the illustrations, it appears that many of the seeds are germinating. You can also seed sparingly as it is still likely that most of the seeds will grow. When over-seeding, one or more of the sprouts may die, with their decayed nutrients supporting the remaining plants. You may also need to thin an area if too many seeds germinate. In the beginning, it may take up to two weeks before the seeds germinate.

11. **Covering** – There are many types of protective products for gardens; feel free to apply any fencing or doming systems as you see necessary for your climate. Fences differ depending on the problem whether it be bugs, animals or other elements of nature.

12. **River Bottom Pea Gravel** – There are literally thousands of types of water or river-based pea gravel in the world. All of it should produce the same end result: enabling vegetation growth. Some river pea gravel will support growth better than others, depending on a variety of factors that include but are not limited to: 1) the river, lake or ocean from which the gravel originates; 2) the geological fault line underlying the rivers, lakes or ocean; 3) the type of life forms in the water; and 4) natural microorganism reproduction tendencies between one gravel type and the next. Since the cost of a bag of river pea gravel is cheap enough to test several types, one should do so. If all produce the same in output, go with the gravel type that you like best visually.

13. **Portability** – Although the system requires some basic setup, it is also completely portable. Neither rock nor sand will decay in your lifetime, so you can always relocate your gravel garden. If you do, it is best to do so in the winter when everything is dead or dormant. At this point, mixing up the gravel will not affect your growing expectations. Simply put the gravel and sand in sturdy bags or containers and relocate.

14. **Green** – Gravel gardening may represent the most efficient use of nature to provide food for people. Gravel and sand are organic and sustainable by nature. This approach eliminates soil degradation, fertilizer contamination and soil consumption. Gravel gardens reduce weeds, water requirements and cost to garden. This method uses materials that are in abundance on the planet.

15. **Organic** – We have consulted the organic certifiers and they tend to feel that this method of gardening can be certified as organic for growers who choose to go through the organic certification process. They also indicate that a method in of itself is not certifiable because someone who uses gravel as the growing medium may still do or add something else that may make it non organic. Each growing operation has to go through the organic certification process to be listed as organic. If you seek to label your gravel garden as organically certified, this method would possibly pass the organic test.

16. **Planting** – Should you want to plant other plants from your local nursery that are already in dirt or soil, you are able to do so. Simply make sure you have enough depth and treat the gravel like dirt and transplant from the pot to the gravel and water. The irrigation system will also impact the dirt, allowing for a sustained and moist environment within the soil. You should initially water potted plants frequently.

17. **Integrating Soil** – If you choose, you can mix soil within the gravel. We have done this to determine growth effectiveness and found that soil that is mixed with gravel tends to provide robust growing environments without adding fertilizers. The irrigation principals apply so the vegetation can still be robust.

18. **Harvesting** – Be careful when picking your crop from a gravel garden. The looseness of the gravel means you have to make sure you don't pull the roots, unless you choose to do so. For most harvesting, we recommend cutting or pruning versus pulling. You can easily de-root a plant.

19. **Troubleshooting** – If the system is not working, here are some common likely causes:
    » Not enough water at the onset – fix by watering.
    » The gravel is too shallow and the outdoor temperatures dries out the gravel bed – fix by adding more gravel to build better insulation from the sun.
    » The lawn fabric doesn't appear to retain the water – fix by doubling up the layers of lawn fabric and/or add a layer of plastic under the lawn fabric. If you add the plastic, punch a few holes in the plastic so that you have some drainage taking place.

Living With Your Gravel Garden

Now that we have gone through the process of how to grow crops in gravel, here is a recap of things to remember and consider.

River Pea Gravel – The entire system is dependent on sourcing the proper type of river pea gravel. This type of gravel is generally available at most nursery retailers. The gravel in large home improvement stores may not be the best, so be sure to shop around. When laying the gravel, keep it at less than three inches, although two inches deep is ideal.

Test First – Before going too widespread, always test your gravel engagements in a small area using multiple types of river bottom pea gravel. You will figure out if your construction of the gravel garden is successful in the three weeks after planting. If you see the sprouts emerging, you are on the right track.

Watering – When properly constructed, your gravel garden should not require too much watering. But always examine the gravel to make sure it has not dried out. When in doubt, water again. If you notice your crops withering, then add water and they should come back. You will need to water more with indoor gravel gardens than outdoor gravel gardens. When you first set up your gravel garden outdoors, water until it floods. You should do this two times a week for the first two weeks. After that water weekly. If it rains often you shouldn't need to water much.

Seeds – The normal seeds purchased at your local garden or grocery store should do well in gravel gardens.

Level – Make sure your planting area is level. If there is a slant, the moisture does not hold properly.

Plastic – Be sure to lay plastic under the fabric. When doing so poke a few holes (two holes every four feet) in the plastic.

Success – Not all things will grow all the time the same way. Although we have had gravel gardens for 15 years, variances can occur. You can always put in more seeds and water more. Although we have not tried it, you can always add fertilizers and compost to the gravel to assist. We have also found that a gravel soil mix is effective as well. Feel free to experiment with gravel in your gardening process.

Cement – Never install a gravel garden directly on cement; always raise the bed above the cement,

Tools

Gravel gardening set-up and maintenance requires the use of three key tools: 1) a shovel for digging the initial trench, 2) metal rakes for weeding any airborne weeds, and 3) stirrups or loop hoes that allow you to dig through the gravel to harvest the plants, roots and all, without disrupting the gravel and fabric underneath. A regular hoe can be used to smooth gravel when constructing your gravel beds. Metal rakes can also pull up any roots if you want to begin to plant other things in a given area.

Gravel Gardening Costs

The materials needed for gravel gardening are basic sand, river pea gravel, and lawn fabric. All of these materials can be relatively inexpensive. A bag of river gravel costs the same as a bag of soil, roughly about $4 to $10 per bag. Gravel lasts a lifetime, while soil degrades each season. Consumers can look at the measurement on the bags of gravel to determine how much gravel to purchase for various space sizes.

Lawn fabric can be purchased in rolls of 25, 50 and 100 feet for less than $10 or $50 per roll. Sand is also cheap at $4 to $6 per bag.

Compared to hydroponic methods, gravel gardening is a fraction of the cost using a fraction of the water. Compared to regular soil gardening, gravel gardening is also a fraction of the cost, as soil needs to be purchased annually and gravel, once purchased, can last for many years to come.

For large farms, the cost can rise somewhat, but when you purchase gravel by the ton, it can cost around $20 to $30 per ton.

Chapter 7
The Business of Geological Agriculture

The Business of Geological Agriculture Intro

To Soil Less™ owns the patent for geological agriculture with 16 claims approved to include creating a gravel garden anywhere in America. With the final patent issued on September 1, 2015, we have outlined the business aspects of geological agriculture.

Why patent something that all of society can use so easily?

- **Misuse** – With thousands of rock types, it is easy to choose untested sedimentary rocks or misconfigure your garden, casting the science into poor light before it even begins.
- **Coordination** – Given the potential applications of gravel gardening, it is important in the first 10 years that the various sub-sectors of gravel gardening develop properly for maximum consumer use and long-term impact.
- **Science** – The creation and advancement of sciences is led by the collection of people who create and oversee the development of the science. Every scientific movement has a lead authority over it and with the science of geological agriculture, To Soil Less™ is the authority having a 20-year head start on the study.
- **Maximum Impact** – The geological agriculture strategic plan is designed for comprehensive integration into society so that all appropriate segments enjoy the benefits that gravel has to offer.

To Soil Less™ invites everyone to use the application of geological agriculture. The *Grown in Gravel* annual manuals are designed for home and community gardeners, not businesses. By buying the manual, the purchaser is authorized to apply geological agriculture concepts in their home and local school environment.

The book on the business of gravel has not been officially written. This section of the book will provide an introduction to the various business applications of geological agriculture. In-depth business grade literature will be developed as the relevant businesses conduct tests in coordination with To Soil Less™. The business world has too much to lose by rushing into an unknown. Many have sought to engage geological agriculture without the proper knowledge, purchasing the wrong type of rock in mass. On the home level, this can cost a few hundred dollars, but this type of mistake on the business level can amount to thousands in losses.

The next few pages outline the 17 sectors of geological agriculture, each representing a sub-industry of activity, business, markets, consumers segments, science projects and more.

The Industries of Geological Agriculture

Geological agriculture is a new science with significant impact to greater society across a variety of segments. The potential is significant because it introduces an all-natural alternative to soil. The entire agriculture industry along with all related sub-components are based on crop production in soil. The advent of geological agriculture offers a new natural alternative to soil. No, you will not see fields of gravel growing corn. But you may see homes, community gardeners and greenhouses using gravel to cultivate crops. You may see real estate developers installing custom-made gravel gardens or new green buildings with gravel gardens on the rooftops and walkways.

The 17 currently identified industries affected by geological agriculture include the following:

1) Academia
2) Big Box Retailers
3) Commercial Farming
4) Farmers Markets
5) Fertilizing Companies
6) International Development
7) Landscapers
8) Medical Marijuana
9) Mining and Distribution
10) Municipal
11) Non-Profits
12) Public Health
13) Publishing
14) Real Estate Development
15) Restaurants
16) Space Exploration
17) Survival and Disaster Relief

Each of the 17 business industries currently use soil in some form or fashion. Gravel provides a sustainable alternative to use in concert with soil. Each of the industries will eventually have new chapters written where geological agriculture concepts are integrated.

In this edition, we provide an overview of each industry. Future editions will include research from relevant entities to further develop the science of geological agriculture for the specific industry. The results on the ongoing study will be published in future editions, expanding the knowledge base for each industry.

Academia

Academia plays a critical role in the development of the science of geological agriculture, as sciences are generally born, studied and developed in institutions of higher learning. Tennessee State University and George Washington University are the first two institutions to study geological agriculture. GWU provides the geological referencing while TSU shares the agricultural aspects. Being the pioneering academic institutions, all research conducted with respect to geological agriculture will be housed at these institutions.

The Lowell School in Washington, DC, was the first elementary school to adopt geological agricultural principals both on the school grounds and in the classroom. The methods of gravel gardening integration at Lowell will serve as a blueprint for applications in other K-12 environments.

Engagement Strategies

1. Collaborate with universities that have both geological and agriculture departments.
2. Seek grant opportunities for K-12 schools and universities to study the effects of gravel gardening in the local environment.
3. Engage in a gravel gardening study and publish the results in the appropriate academic journals.
4. Develop textbooks and curriculums of coursework in geological agriculture.
5. Develop a minor within any number of departments from agriculture, to earth sciences, to engineering and business.

As a study, geological agriculture is designed initially more as a minor than a major. Given the broad spectrum of impact, a student can major in business and minor in geo-ag and then help private sector companies leverage the full impact of gravel sciences. Another student can major in civil engineering but minor in geoag engineering and incorporate gravel sciences in building and infrastructure design.

In the K-12 environment, gravel gardening will find a home outdoors in the school gardens, inside the science class and possibly turned into a school business where students run a gravel grown farmers market. In the Lowell pre-primary classroom, preschool kids snack on pea shoots sprouts grown in the gravel on the windowsill during the winter, enabling students to snack on produce year round.

Big Box Retailers

A variety of consumer products will be made available through retailers related to gravel gardening. The initial products will be the gravel grow cups and the paperback book *River Stone Grow Plants 2018 Edition*. The ideal retailers are those like Ace Hardware that already sell the proper gravel. We recommend the KolorScape Gravilla brand of river pea gravel distributed through Old Castle.

Generally speaking, garden centers or home improvement retailers have the gravel and sand required to build and manage a successful gravel garden. Most garden centers have the basic gravel gardening supplies for consumers to construct their own gravel gardens at home.

The two primary items that garden center retailers don't have is the *know how* of gravel gardening and the introductory sampler gravel grow cups for consumers to use at home. Equipped with the book and pre-seeded gravel grow cups, consumers can witness the fundamentals and then expand outdoors. Some retailers will create gravel gardening sections in their stores where consumers can go to one area for all of their gravel gardening needs.

Additional gravel gardening products planned include:

1. Guides, books and encyclopedias of gravel types around the world
2. Gravel fertility testing equipment
3. Proven gravel alternatives of various colors
4. Gravel and soil mixtures
5. Gravel, soil and fertilizer mixtures
6. Gravel grow cups (image shown)
7. Gravel garden survival kit
8. Gravel science lab in a box
9. Starter gravel garden kit
10. Balcony gravel kit – 20 lbs.
11. Gravel installation services

Gravel Grow Cup
Retail Box

Old Takoma Ace Hardware - Gravel Garden 2015

The Old Takoma Ace Hardware in Takoma Park, MD, is the flagship gravel gardening store with a 4 x 4 foot gravel garden. This year, we experimented with a variety of flowers, but it was the beans that were most impressive. With a fence added, the beans grew, creating a 3-foot tall wall of beans. The Ace Hardware staff was able to harvest the beans three times over the course of the summer.

String Beans

String Beans

Old Takoma Ace Hardware - Gravel Garden 2016

The Ace Hardware gravel garden in Takoma Park, MD, demonstrated that mums return with a vengeance from the prior year. In 2015 a small mum plant started and died. By the fall of 2016, the mum returned nearly three times the size as shown below. The gladiolus in the gravel grow cup grew about five feet tall in the 16-ounce cup, while peas and gladiolus flowered outdoors.

Mums – June 6

Gladiolus – June 6

Peas – June 6

Gladiolus – June 24

Gladiolus

Mums – October 4

Commercial Farming

Commercials farmers should explore the benefits for geological agriculture within the context of broad crop production. Given the $50,000 per acre retrofit cost, it is unlikely that an entire acre will be converted to gravel. Additionally, row farming, greenhouse farming and organic farming will likely adopt aspects of gravel gardening.

Similar to the gardens developed in this manual, farmers can make 100-foot long rows 4 to 5 feet wide of the desired crop. Once the best gravel is identified, the benefits of crop cultivation with gravel is the ongoing reduction in the cost of fertilizers. For greenhouses, gravel presents a sustainable reusable option for cultivating seedlings.

Some large-scale farmers may opt to leverage "gravel water" in lieu of converting large areas to gravel gardens. Gravel water for agriculture is the process of integrating gravel into the irrigation cycle. This is done by passing water through large containers of gravel before using the water for crops. Those who can allow water to sit in gravel for a few weeks will benefit from the constant leaching of gravel into the water. After a few weeks of sitting in gravel, the gravel water will be higher in nutrients for crops. Depending on how farmers construct the gravel water holding container, natural rain water can also fill the container, limiting the need for well or city water.

A key consideration for commercial farmers is the harvest methodologies applied to the crops grown. Commercial gravel gardens are more designed for hand harvest versus machine or tractor harvest. With some harvesting machines, the gravel make kick up into the machine and damage the blades. In time, engineers will help solve that issue.

Farmers Market

The entrepreneurial gardener will enjoy the benefits of geological agriculture as each week they will literally see their profits grow. On day one, a dry gravel grow cup or pot can be sold for $5 per cup. Should you add water and wait a week, the plants could be about an inch high and sell for $6 a cup or pot. After two weeks like with the beans shown below, you could sell the cup of five or six bean plants for $7 a cup or more. Basically for about $8 in supplies for the set of 11 bean cups below, about $77 or more can be made at the local farmers market. Should gardeners follow all of the instructions of gravel gardening, they could likely create an indoor gravel grow farm 365 days a year and consistently provide local consumers with fresh sustainable produce.

Gardeners seeking to sell gravel grown crops in a farmers market must inform To Soil Less of the crops grown and gravel type used. This is to identify the gravel type and add it to the national list of ideal gravel types, retail locations and source river. Gardeners should also test the target crop through a full cycle before moving forward with consumer engagement. The gardener should grow a full set of the desired crop in a similar fashion as what is shown below to check for consistency, plant color and vitality with the gravel used. All river rocks are different, affecting their ability to grow crops where one type is better than another. The gardener should watch the plants grow as far as they can, timing how long it will last and observing how it evolves so that you better communicate with consumers about what to expect. Gravel is new, so do not presume anything. The best way is to watch a complete cycle, empty the contents, rinse out the cup and start over and re-seed. Then watch the crop for the second and maybe the third round to have first-hand knowledge before selling to consumers.

All gravel retail locations should have the book on gravel gardening. Without the book, it is easy to miss a step, resulting in poor performance. The outdoor methodology is much different than the indoor gravel grow cups, for example, which is why consumers need the book to adopt gravel techniques properly at home.

Squash

Peas

Mustard Greens

Beans

Fertilizing Companies

From the onset, some assert that gravel gardening methodologies encroach on the space of fertilizing companies and can serve to cannibalize chemical fertilizers. In one sense this is true, but in another sense a whole new market is open to big fertilizers. Given the types of gravel, some common river rocks don't perform as well as others for specific plant types. Fertilizing companies will begin to develop fertilizers, natural and synthetic, to aid and amplify the effects of crops grown in gravel.

Although some 30 to 40 plant types have been tested in gravel, trees, shrubs and common field crops such as soy have not proven effective in gravel to date. Fertilizing companies will need to make compounds that will maximize crop production in gravel where gravel alone doesn't do it, especially for large-scale common field crops.

Fertilizing companies may find use from gravel water as well given its fertilizing nature. Gravel water is the foundation of the Campbell Equation of Water + River Rock = Plant Food. All of geological agriculture is predicated on the gravel water constantly producing nutrients for root systems. Further fertilizing opportunities may arise as research on using gravel water in soil is explored.

Big fertilizing companies have the resources and capacity to source the world's best gravel and provide it to consumers in the similar fashion that fertilizer is provided. With gravel being cheaper in cost than the development of synthetic fertilizers, big fertilizer can gain financially in adopting geological agriculture techniques. Humanity has studied soil-grown crops for thousands of years. Gravel sciences is at its debut. Big fertilizer can supply consumers for decades various types of crop gravel and associated supplements.

Gravel enrichment farms can be developed where you lay gravel beds for the purpose of enriching the gravel. This is accomplished by creating a standard gravel bed that is about six inches deep and using the bed as a composting location. After a season of composting with super fertilizers such as cow or chicken manure or common fertilizers such as everyday organic waste in the household, the gravel will become stronger. The decay and composting under the rain and heat coupled with the activity of the worms and slugs will amplify the impact of the gravel garden the following season. This gravel can be rinsed and dried in the sun and packaged to sell to consumers.

Big industry fertilizing companies have three overall ways to develop markets integrating geological agriculture techniques as described: 1) gravel supplements, 2) gravel water and 3) gravel enrichment farms for crop gravel.

International Development

The natural tendency when hearing about gravel gardening is its use in places like Ethiopia and other parts of Africa where access to viable soil is limited. Droughts, water shortages and depleting soils pose significant challenges around the world and gravel sciences can aid in addressing some of the issues through research and training.

Research is needed in each country to determine the best locally available gravel. Once the best gravel is identified, non-governmental organizations (NGOs) and donors can adopt programming to send trucks of the appropriate gravel, sand, seeds and instructions to villages, installing and training people how to assemble and manage gravel gardens at home and in local businesses. Development agencies can integrate gravel gardening training into their instruction of workshops that they conduct for community support, showing families how to develop sustainable gardens that can provide supplemental produce at home year round.

In the international development arena, geological agriculture touches small business development, community development, women's development and obviously agriculture and food security. With a properly constructed gravel garden, give a family seeds once and they can harvest and keep the seeds for the next season. Sharing this approach and methodology to countries that could use alternative methods towards sustainable food production and security could represent a step closer in addressing global food security.

The world has a lot to offer with respect to geological agriculture as each country has a variety of rivers and bodies of water with varying types of sedimentary material likely capable of supporting plant life. Some parts of the world will have natural deposits of the best gravel in the world for crop production. Once global geologists begin to identify the specific chemical composition of gravel that produces crops well, the global geological survey is able to identify the rivers and land deposits that likely possess the sedimentary material for healthy crop production.

Beans

Lettuce

Landscapers

As community interest in gravel gardening increases, landscapers will play an important role in installing and teaching gravel gardening techniques to homeowners. Landscapers will be able to help the busy American who would rather pay someone to come set up their gravel garden and maintain it versus reading the manual. Fortunately, many Americans love having their lawns done for them, so showing landscapers how to upsell a gravel garden should earn additional sources of revenue for landscaping companies.

Landscapers will be trained and certified by To Soil Less™ to test local gravel types and to install a variety of gravel gardens for consumer, commercial and municipal use. Landscapers currently have these market segments as customers. Over time, landscaping companies will become the focal point for gravel proliferation in most communities as it is sometimes easier to call someone than to do it yourself. Upon installation, the landscaping company will provide the latest edition of the manual so that the knowledge of gravel gardening is available to the consumer after the landscaper leaves.

Eventually, To Soil Less™ will partner with a variety of landscaping companies in growth markets to train staff on gravel gardening techniques. To Soil Less invites all landscapers to learn the nuance of gravel gardening so that they can maximize the benefits of this growth market. The gravel garden on cement below is a configuration that landscapers may find popular in urban settings.

Pea shoots, beans, peas and wheatgrass

Garden beans

Medical Marijuana

For residents in states where legalized, research with medical marijuana seeds in gravel is in its infancy with limited comprehensive testing. The indoor photos under basic light on the left below depict emergence after day 7 and by day 30 some of the seedlings grew as tall as eight inches. Now that the plant has germinated and is established, it is possible that they can grow to full term, similar to other crops grown in gravel. The plant outdoors on the right was planted from seed on April 1 while the photo was taken May 14, 2015. The few experts that have weighed in have indicated that 70% of the cost is getting the plant to germinate.

After 7 days

After 9 days

After 30 days

Medical Marijuana

This plant was removed after the pictures were taken below due to residence relocation. Notice that there are nine leaves where usually there are seven. Additional experiments need to be taken but so far it appears that gravel can grow medical marijuana.

Medical Marijuana

For places where marijuana growing is legal, below are some bad examples of pot seeds growing in gravel. Germination tends to be easy and quick, usually sprouting with 10 days. The plant will also enter into its budding phase to a degree in the gravel grow cup. The gravel does appear to cultivate seedlings until they become a male, enabling growers to discard male plants sooner. Had the plants matured with high-powered indoor lights, the outcome may differ than shown on this page and likely resemble the outdoor research outcome. Should growers refine the process with better lights and seeds, the likelihood of geological agricultural concept benefiting the medical marijuana industry is high. These plants died shortly after the budding process started. They were also un-attended for a period of time. This application will tend to complement germination more for marijuana than full plant development.

Medical Marijuana

Unlike the medical marijuana experiment of 2015, the version below shows that seeds planted on July 1, 2017 are up and growing by July 15, and entering its budding phase by September 15 or 2 ½ months later. This rate of growth is on par with some hydroponic methods but lacks the cost. The shorter plant visible up until August 10 grew into a male plant and was removed upon signs that the plant was in fact male. By September 10 visible white hairs expanding from each leaf layer continues to suggest that the plant is budding up, so to speak. Like the experiments of 2015, the images in this book will not show the results of the budding process below as this 2018 edition was published in the fall of 2017 and the last photos below were taken on September 27, 2017 with a few more months left before harvest. A larger image of the budding process is found in the gallery section at the end of the book.

July 15

July 26

August 10

Sept 17

Oct 4

Mining and Distribution

Research will test and identify the gravel from the major gravel distributors in the United States and certify the gravel before it is recommended for gardening. Not all gravel produces crops equally. With hundreds of rivers in the United States, the variability of gravel type, color and impact is significant. Over time, To Soil Less™ and academic partners will work with identified excavating companies that dredge and mine gravel usually from rivers to figure out where the "good" gravel comes from. So far, the Tennessee River and Susquehanna River gravel are the best gravel that have been tested in producing crops. To Soil Less™ refers to tested and proven gravel as *crop gravel*.

With testing and partnerships, the To Soil Less™ crop gravel seal of approval will go on the packaging of participating distributors. On the backside packaging of bags of river pea gravel, the space is usually left empty. Participating distributors can also print simple gravel gardening instructions on the back of the packaging so that consumers can purchase and construct gravel gardens on their own.

As more research is conducted, new blends of gravel and other materials may emerge as we may find that gravel mined from Pacific Ocean inlet rivers prove to be different than the gravel from the rivers of the Atlantic Ocean when trying to grow a specific crop. As more types of gravel are identified as crop gravel, the difference will become color, allowing consumers to select gravel garden types based on color and style of their yards and landscaping. Another difference may be the growing impact for specific seed types.

New York investment banker Darrell Smith sees crop gravel as a new commodities market where types and grades of crop gravel are graded and traded. Grade A and B crop gravel may become the cornerstone of rooftops across all schools and buildings, increasing the overall demand for gravel and sand. It will be some time before geological agriculture graduates to the level of a commodities market, so check back in the future to see where we are.

Municipal

Recognizing the municipal challenges with landscaping and agriculture, To Soil Less™ has developed a framework for municipalities seeking to benefit from the attributes of geological agriculture and address food deserts.

1. Reduce the use of water in the upkeep of new city endeavors appropriate for gravel gardening.
    a) Train city contractors and architects on how to set up gravel gardens in a variety of city configurations
    b) Develop custom elements to facilitate ease of use for the city

2. Encourage city homeowners to develop gravel gardens to help grow their own food and conserve water in food deserts.
    a) Disseminate information through appropriate channels
    b) Host demonstrations
    c) Potentially provide homeowner incentives

3. Encourage business owners to incorporate gravel into their operations as a certifiable technique for city requirements.
    a) Train landscaping companies to offer gravel services in homes
    b) Train real estate developers to add gravel features in new home developments, condominiums and apartments (including roof-top gravel gardens)
    c) Encourage young people to start businesses on building and servicing gravel gardens
    d) Provide incentives for agriculture companies using gravel

4. Develop plans for schools and colleges (public & private) to grow crops in gravel and study the use of gravel.
    a) Host training sessions for schools and community organizations
    b) Use our staff and resources to directly assist entities with gravel growth system start-up and maintenance
    c) Work with local universities to test the advancement of gravel agriculture, as well as study the positive economic and potential educational impacts of wide-spread utilization of gravel-based growth systems vs. traditional, high-water volume dependent landscaping and agricultural techniques

These municipal applications should be done in concert with To Soil Less to help cities avoid the pitfalls of gravel gardening, namely misconfiguration and wrong gravel types.

Non-Profits

The non-profit community can adopt geological agriculture methodologies for each of the prior sectors discussed. Non-profits are supported largely by grants. There are many grants related to sustainable agriculture, innovation, as well as school and community gardening that are ideal for non-profit organizations. Non-profit collaboration with both universities and the private sector will help deliver the benefits of gravel gardening to appropriate populations. Whether overseas in developing nations or in the United States in developing communities, gravel gardening takes a step closer in reducing the amount of food deserts in urban environments.

In 2015, the To Soil Less™ team developed the notion of providing gravel grow cups to the poor and homeless. A gravel grow cup with a pack of alfalfa sprouts from Botanical Interests can provide alfalfa snacks every 14 days for a year. Should the poor or homeless have three or four gravel grow cups in rotation, they will be able to keep a steady supply of edibles to help provide some sort of nutrition. Botanical Interests seed packs are voluminous, enabling many planting from one pack. In a 9-oz. cup, one pack of seeds can last a for about 12 rounds of planting and harvesting.

Alfalfa sprouts, lettuce and broccoli sprouts

Non-profits can work to provide gravel grow cups to the poor and homeless in their communities to assist in providing access to the nutritional value found in the micro greens and sprouts.

Public Health

The public health aspects of geological agriculture are only theoretical today. Tomorrow gravel water may prove to aid in human health in the same way it has been proven to aid in plant health. Humans and vegetation are very similar, requiring water, air, sunlight and food. We know that the minerals that are leached at the highest rates in gravel water are potassium, copper and silica. The question is, what do they do for the body?

According to WebMd.com, "Potassium is a mineral that plays many critical roles in the body. Food sources of potassium include fruits (especially dried fruits), cereals, beans, milk, and vegetables. Potassium is used for treating and preventing low potassium levels. It is also used to treat high blood pressure and prevent stroke. Some people use it to treat high levels of calcium, a type of dizziness called Menière's disease, thallium poisoning, insulin resistance, symptoms of menopause, and infantcolic. It is also used for allergies, headaches, acne, alcoholism, Alzheimer's disease, confusion, arthritis, blurred vision, cancer, chronic fatigue syndrome, an intestinal disorder called colitis, constipation, dermatitis, bloating, fever, gout, insomnia, irritability, mononucleosis, muscle weakness, muscular dystrophy, stress, and with medications as treatment for myasthenia gravis."

The mineral second most prevalent in gravel water is copper. WebMd.com share that, "Copper is a mineral. It is found in many foods, particularly in organ meats, seafood, nuts, seeds, wheat bran cereals, grain products, and cocoa products. The body stores copper mostly in the bones and muscles. The liver regulates the amount of copper that is in the blood. Copper is used as medicine.

Copper is used for treating copper deficiency and the anemia it may cause. Having too little copper (copper deficiency) is rare. It sometimes occurs in people who get too much zinc from diet or supplements, have intestinal bypass surgery, or are fed by feeding tubes. Malnourished infants can also have copper deficiency. Copper is also used for improving wound healing, and treating osteoarthritis and brittle bones (osteoporosis). There is no evidence that people who eat a normal diet need copper supplements. Not even athletes need extra copper if they have a good diet."

The final mineral on the rise in gravel water is silica. WebMd.com does not say much but Google it and you will find that silica too is good for human health. Some assert that silica is the most important trace mineral for human health. He claims that silica is used sometimes to get rid of ticks, fleas and other parasites that seem to be around all spring and summer.

On the surface we seem to have an opportunity for further research to positively affect human health. The science of geological agriculture will affect humanity in ways unknown as gravel types differ worldwide. What cures are really in the rocks from the sea?

Publishing

The publishing of books related to gravel gardening will grow as the science evolves and expands. To Soil Less™ issues the annual edition of geological agriculture, adding the discoveries gained during the year. To date, this 260-page 2018 edition describes what is known so far as it relates to geological agriculture. The first edition was developed in 2013, but was not made available to the general public. The 2018 edition is the first edition shared widely with the public.

As outlined in the business sectors overview, there are 17 sub-industries to come with geological agriculture applications. Each will need its own literature to specify use, refinement and maximization within the specific industry. The books published by engineers for building and infrastructure will differ from those published by biologists. The biology of plants grown in gravel is a book in of itself, but so is the book on the best edibles to grow in gravel at restaurants. With many restaurants growing their own food, at some point the gravel for restaurants book will outline how to integrate gravel gardening for meals.

Publishing will come in many forms with gravel sciences from academic white papers to comprehensive textbooks and paperbacks. Online versions will emerge as consumers document their experience with cultivating crops in gravel. Eventually an encyclopedia of geological agriculture will chart the best gravel types in each country along with listing the crops most likely to grow and thrive with the various gravel types.

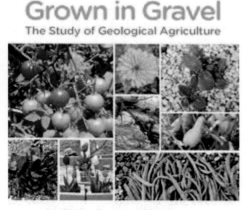

Real Estate Developers

Gravel gardening or gravel sciences techniques can play a role in construction projects of the future. The primary areas of construction where gravel gardens can participate include the following:

- **Rooftop Garden Design** – Rooftops can become full garden-producing environments while maintaining smart water usage, conservation and runoff.
- **Balcony Garden Design** – Balconies can now be designed with permanent sustainable growing environments for condo and apartment owners.
- **Lobby Landscape Design** – Lobby areas and indoor walkways can be designed with attractive custom design gravel gardens of a variety of plant types.
- **School Landscaping** – School playgrounds and grounds can be designed with gravel gardens for education, sustainable crop production for the school and in-class experiments.
- **Home Landscaping Design** – Homeowners can now have custom gravel gardens integrated into the landscape design for a variety of foliage and crop types to suit the tastes of the owners.
- **Commercial Landscaping Design** – Public outdoor spaces can adapt gravel gardens as attractive ways to control soil erosion and water runoff while cultivating usable crops.
- **LEED Certifications** – Because of its attributes, geological agricultural methods can aid builders in developing more sustainable construction projects.

To integrate gravel gardening techniques in real estate, To Soil Less™ and partner academic institutions will identify the best gravel for commercial use between the currently identified gravel and those found in the location of the real estate projects. Working with the American Institute of Architectural (AIA), commercial architects will be trained on how to build and construct the various custom gravel garden configurations consistent with the various needs of consumers; develop gravel garden marketing brochures; and train real estate brokers and others on how to upsell the gravel garden feature to home owners and buyers.

With real estate developers, the goal of training is to enable them to offer gravel gardens as a green feature when building new homes and developments. Given the pursuits of LEED certification and organic certification, gravel assists real estate developers in their eco-friendly properties. Research and collaborative engineering is needed to properly develop gravel installation standards.

.

Gravel and the LEED Rating Systems

According to the U.S. Green Building Council, LEED, or Leadership in Energy & Environmental Design, is a green building certification program that recognizes best-in-class building strategies and practices. There are five LEED rating systems that address multiple project types as shown below. Within each type of construction project or rating system, geological agricultural (GA) sciences can aid in the pursuit of sustainable construction and building design with items listed below outlining the primary support areas for each rating system. To date, no developer has attempted to use geological agriculture concepts in building design.

1	2	3	4	5
	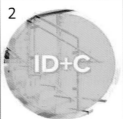	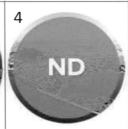	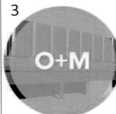	
Building Design and Construction	**Interior Design and Construction**	**Building Operations and Maintenance**	**Neighborhood Development**	**Homes**
GA Science supports:	**GA Science** integrates:	**GA Science** reduces:	**GA Science** improves:	**GA Science** provides:
✓ Rooftops gardens ✓ Balcony gardens ✓ Landscaping enhancements	✓ Innovative and sustainable building engineering and architectural design principals in construction	✓ Materials and resources ✓ Management and maintenance	✓ Sustainable outdoor spaces ✓ Gardening and crop management aesthetics	✓ A permanent sustainable growing environment ✓ Outdoor and indoor crop development options

Should developers and architects seek innovation, geological agriculture techniques can aid in attaining credits across a variety of LEED credit categories for neighborhood development as described.

Green infrastructure & buildings
credits reduce the environmental consequences of the construction and operation of buildings and infrastructure.

Green Infrastructure & Buildings

Geological Agriculture Techniques can be:

1. Applied to urban roof design
2. Integrated onto a balcony
3. Showcased in the lobby area
4. Designed for outdoor public places
5. Developed as a permanent growing environment

Neighborhood pattern & design
credits emphasize compact, walkable, vibrant, mixed-use neighborhoods with good connections to nearby communities.

Neighborhood Pattern & Design

Geological Agriculture Techniques can be:

1. Integrated along pathways
2. Provide attractive sustainable gardens
3. Showcases sustainable flowering plants
4. Provide public growing spaces with minimal weeding

Gravel Gardening LEED Credit Categories

Geological agriculture techniques can aid in attaining credits across a variety of LEED credit categories as numbered below for the specific category.

Integrative Process requirements, while not a credit category, promote reaching across disciplines to incorporate diverse team members during the pre-design period.

Materials and Resources credits encourage using sustainable building materials and reducing waste. Indoor environmental quality credits promote better indoor air quality and access to daylight and views.

Energy and atmosphere credits promote better building energy performance through innovative strategies.

Integrative Process

Geological Agriculture Promotes:

1. Integrating engineering, geology and agriculture into building design
2. Conserving energy, water and costs for sustainable vegetation

Materials and Resources

Geological Agriculture Encourages:

1. Using available construction materials for sustainable crop maintenance
2. Reducing waste of common materials such as sand and gravel

Energy and Atmosphere

Geological Agriculture Reduces:

1. Energy related to weeding, fertilizing and turning soil
2. Energy related to drought prevention and watering
3. Energy

Geological agriculture techniques can aid in attaining credits across a variety of LEED credit categories as numbered below for the specific category.

Innovation credits address sustainable building expertise as well as design measures not covered under the five LEED credit categories.

Water efficiency credits promote smarter use of water, inside and out, to reduce potable water consumption.

Sustainable sites credits encourage strategies that minimize the impact on ecosystems and water resources.

Innovation

Geological Agriculture Addresses:

1. Innovation in sustainable green gardening and vegetation management design
2. Innovation in using basic construction materials to produce foods

Water Efficiency

Geological Agriculture Uses:

1. Over 50% less watering than conventional gardening
2. Condensation principals to create water in hot climates

Sustainable Sites

Geological Agriculture Creates:

1. A fertilizer- and soil-free, all-natural permanent growing environment
2. An appreciating ecosystem with each year's decay adding organic material
3. Gardens that don't need manual watering

Restaurants

Across America, restaurants are growing their own food, especially the core items of lettuce, spinach, kale, greens, tomatoes, cucumbers and potatoes. Some even have caught the sprout and micro greens bandwagon. Gravel gardening can play a role with specialty restaurants, serving as a sustainable growing environment for food grown for customers.

Restaurant owners will need to understand gravel gardening concepts for best output in the kitchen. Assigned growing areas should be equipped with natural and artificial lights for controlled growth. Key to restaurant usage of gravel grow cups or containers for sprouts and micro greens is establishing a proper planting cycle for consumer demand and properly cleaning and reusing the gravel grow cups for ongoing production. Special cleaning and sifting strainers will be need to separate the roots, sand and gravel once the growing cycle is complete.

With the concept of gravel gardening being new, To Soil Less™ recommends that restaurant owners that grow their own crops test their local gravel types using the applications in this manual to identify the best gravel for the crops of choice. In the gravel grow cups below, wheat grass is ready for juicing, while the alfalfa sprouts and bean mix are ready of the salad. The peas shoots sprouts are good right out of the cup, providing a healthily fresh snack appetizer prior to the main course.

Space Exploration

News Channel 8 anchor Melanie Hastings of Washington, DC, asked if geological agriculture concepts could be used in outer space. The answer is: likely. The fundamentals of the composition of the rock and its durability do not change in space. The air inside a space shuttle, on a space station or on a colony provides breathable oxygen, which already contains nitrogen. Oxygen as we know it is 19% oxygen and 80% nitrogen. The presence of nitrogen in the oxygen would make the space environment where humans live the same as on Earth. As long as you have air, strong plant lights and moisture, you can have a gravel garden. Given the range of customization available, a variety of configurations can make growing with gravel in space efficient.

As previously discussed, the presence of heat on gravel creates moisture within gravel. With moisture, The Campbell Equation kicks in and the growth process begins. With heat generating moisture, should proper engineers participate in the development, it would be fairly simple to construct a sustainable gravel farm in space using the ambient heat of the space facility itself to create irrigation absent of outside water.

For micro greens, sprouts and legumes such as the protein-rich families of peas, beans and nuts, the nitrogen fixation characteristics of these plant types has made them capable of growing well in gravel. Green beans, kidney beans, garbanzo beans, sugar snap peas, as well as alfalfa and lentils should all do well in gravel as long as you have the right type of rock. For space exploration, we would tests gravel from river deposits around the world to determine which gravel type is most reliable at crop production.

The bean mix micro greens was left to grow in low-level light for a month and forgotten. As you see below, the bean mix has grown more than two feet in one small 9-oz. cup. Deliberate systems to maximize performance will enable the gravel to produce plants at even a better rate than what you see below. Should the space travel include standard good plant lights then crop production can be permanent.

Space Exploration

Geological agriculture or gravel gardening is a relatively simple process in which to engage. You simply need to configure the growing environment to harness the nutrients within the DNA of the gravel by controlling the amount of water. With NASA on Mars, we are assuming that water will not be available. Therefore, we would need to design a venting system to harness heat exhaust to blow the heat in a grow room or greenhouse in a controlled fashion. As long as a grow room is heated at 100 to 120 degrees, then moisture will be created within the gravel and nutrients will be released. The sun shines on Mars too, I suspect, so the grow room would need to be like a greenhouse for maximum impact so that the natural Mars sunlight does its part to feed the plants light. The heat will take care of the water and the rocks will take care of the food. After that, all you need are seeds.

Experimenting will be required to identify the best gravel on Earth. There are thousands of sedimentary rock. We currently use two types from a test population of about eight in America. The best so far comes from the Tennessee River and the Susquehanna River in Maryland. In that this application is for life in space or on Mars, we want to provide not only the best gravel type, but also be certain of which of the sub-elements are best. For example, within the Maryland river pea gravel, there are about 7 to 12 different types of rock. We know that in combination they work well to produce crops, but which of the specific rocks work best relative to the rest? Theoretically a concentrated combination of 2 or 3 rock types may produce the most optimal output. We will need to experiment some to determine the optimal mix of gravel suitable for quick and efficient production for fresh produce in space.

There are three basic approaches to date with respect to use and delivery in space. There is the individual pack, the space station greenhouse gravel farm and the planetary colony gravel garden. The individual pack would be 4 to 6 gravel grow cups that would occupy the size of a shoe box with each cup weighing about one pound each. Each astronaut could have one in his/her living space using a small light and about ½ cup of water per week per cup. This is ideal for the trip to a space station or planet. After six days the astronaut would be able to eat produce daily for years.

Within a space station greenhouse, there are two versions: rows of cups and/or square feet versions. The greenhouse rows of cups within the gravel farm would be designed where about 200 pounds of gravel or four bags is used to develop rows of gravel grow cups to make about 200 cups. The station gravel greenhouse gardens can also be set up in square feet planting areas. The square foot of a gravel garden weighs about 10 to 20 pounds depending on what you want to grow, temperature and moisture control. The more controlled the environment the less weight per square foot. The colony gravel garden would be the same as the square foot version but bigger, where the garden may be configured 2 x 100 feet. In this case you would need a few thousand pounds.

Survival and Disaster Relief

The basics of how a survivalist would use gravel gardening techniques was discussed in the Alternative Applications section where you take the sand, rocks and shells from the ocean and configure them into a gravel garden. The missing component is the air-tight seed pack of micro greens, sprouts and legumes that can grow within days to get needed protein.

The business of survival is also affected with geological agriculture. First we have the seed companies who can now develop survival seeds kits. Organizations like the Red Cross and FEMA can disburse seeds and instructions in water-proof packs for wilderness preparedness. As long as a person is equipped with the survival seed kit, then when lost on a deserted island or in the wilderness, the ocean or river can provide more than just fish.

A secondary aspects with disaster relief is the shipments of gravel grow cups as both for preparedness and relief. With preparedness, households who prepare for the worst can stock up on gravel grow cups with the proper seed packs. A pack of micro greens from Botanical Interests can provide food for a year or longer in one cup. As long as you have 6 to 12 gravel grow cups per person in a household, you can have a foot tall meal daily of pea shoots micro greens for a year. The photo on the right is a pea shoots micro greens gravel grow cup, growing at Ace Hardware in Washington, DC. Store staff have it for snacks. Imagine what the lost and hungry can have with seeds and gravel knowledge. With disaster relief, in the future aid can also come with six packs of gravel grow cups in a box with six seed packs included.

Pea shoots

When relief agencies provide the meals, they can also provide quick growing gardening packs for ongoing nutrition wherever people may find themselves when struck with natural and man-made disasters. A six pack of the above pea shoots will give you six plants like that to eat daily for an entire year. A whole new approach to relief emerges with geological agriculture. And let us not forget the potential benefits of gravel water.

The Business of Gravel Summary

The business of gravel gardening is in its infancy in 2017 with academic institutions and retailers just coming on board. It will take decades for the various segments of geological agriculture to be fulfilled. This 2018 edition incorporates the business of gravel as a blueprint for ways to integrate geological techniques for those seeking to adopt gravel gardening at home or elsewhere.

We have reviewed 17 sub-sectors of geological agriculture, each with its own nuances, applications and perspectives. Over the next decade advances within each sector will be accumulated and shared with the greater population. During this time, business activity will be closely monitored, studied and refined. Practitioners and gravel gardening business enthusiasts should email questions@tosoilless.com when engaging in any business activity.

Zinnias

Appendices

Gravel Sciences Education Introduction

To Soil Less™ seeks to work with K–12, as well as colleges and universities to study, test and experiment with the science and nutrition of gravel gardening. Each year, TSL issues the next edition of geological agriculture. Given that geological agriculture is a new science, there a new discoveries each year, providing new content to share. All may contribute to the next year's gravel gardening manual by sending photos and study results to questions@tosoilless.com

Two bodies of work have been prepared to initiate the experimentation of gravel sciences in academia;

1)   University Academic Foundation of Discovery

1)   K-12 Experiments

Academic Foundation

Geological agriculture is the process of cultivating and growing crops exclusively in a gravel or rock environment. The relevant work summary below outlines related studies prior to geo-ag that is similar to gravel gardening.

Relevant Work Summary

1.   **Missouri gravel bed** store bare root trees
2.   **Agrogeology** is the method of using rock in soil as fertilizers
3.   **Remineralization** is the process of using rock dust as fertilizers

These three methods of gardening provide an academic foundation that rocks can play a role in agriculture. Agrogeology uses rocks in soil and rock dust is put in soil with remineralization. Both use rock or rock-like materials in soil for the cultivation process as a natural fertilizer. The Missouri gravel bed states that crops are not cultivated in gravel, but bare tree roots can be sustained in gravel over the winter. This suggest that rocks have sustainment properties.

These three methods substantiate the foundation that rocks have nutrients. Geological agriculture takes these notions a step further by using "rocks only" to grow crops.

Geological Agriculture Academic Foundation

Scope of Study

Geoagriculture studies the effects of rock, primarily sedimentary, on vegetation roots systems. Within the process is the study of water and its effect on sand and gravel. The nitrogen cycle process is included in the study as the source of nitrogen is critical in plant development. Atmospheric conditions play a role and the impact of the atmosphere can affect nitrogen fixation with the gravel. Root systems development, micro biological analysis and plant nutrient analysis are also included in this study.

Geological considerations are paramount as there are many types of rock on the planet with many seemingly having the ability to support plant growth. A host of agriculture realities are included in the study with considerations on growth rates, nutrient transfer, sustainability and resilience with respect to growing crops. Analysis and studies related to the decaying process are needed to reveal the annual effect of enrichment within the gravel system. Other analysis may be required.

Implications of Study

Defining and amplifying the ability of using rocks to grow crops absent of soil, fertilizers and daily watering can have a significant impact on the agriculture landscape. Conservation, sustainability and resiliency are achieved simultaneously with gravel agriculture. With the primary growing material being rock instead of soil, the nutrients that are leached from the rock should come from that rock for decades.

Gravel agriculture can assist with climate change effects, food security issues, farming practices, urban produce, green building designs, landscaping, sustainable agriculture, environmental conservation and job creation.

Terms

Geoagriculture – The study of rocks to grow vegetation
Geoag – The abbreviated term for geoagriculture
Gravel agriculture – The application of gravel gardening techniques in commercial and residential landscaping environments
Gravel gardening – The process of using rocks to cultivate vegetation

Geological Agriculture – Unanswered Questions

Geological agriculture is in its infancy so there are many questions not yet fully answered and explored. The questions below represents some key questions that the study of geoag seeks to answer. All researchers seeking to expand upon the study of geoag should first read this manual to provide the foundation of what we know so far. The questions below are for you to explore and answer on behalf of the science:

1. Does all river-based gravel around the world provide the same benefit?
2. What rock types have shown the best results?
3. Can this really produce for a lifetime?
4. Is there any structural loss with the rocks?
5. What is it about the rocks specifically that enable nutritional transfer?
6. How far do roots travel in gravel compared to root development in soil?
7. How long does water store in the system before it dries out completely?
8. What are the effects of the decaying process on the health of the gravel bed?
9. Can the sand gravel filtering characteristics have filtering effects on sea water and gray water?
10. How is fertilizer absorbed?
11. Where does the nitrogen come from?
12. Why are there inconsistencies?
13. What is the best balance of moisture with the gravel for best growth?
14. What crops grow best in which types of gravel?
15. How does the growth rate in gravel compare to the growth rate in soil?
16. What is the most precise range of reduction in water use between gravel gardening and traditional gardening?
17. What is the nutritional impact of commonly grown vegetables and fruits?
18. What is the potential economic impact of gravel agriculture on society?
19. Where is the best gravel found?
20. What are the effects of natural fertilizers such as peanuts and compost?
21. What at the effects of synthetic fertilizers?
22. What are the greenhouse effects?
23. How do bugs, worms and other pests interface with vegetation in gravel environments?
24. How does gravel perform in commercial applications?
25. What is the impact of heat on rock?
26. Is moisture created when it is higher than 100 degrees and the depth is deeper than 2.5 inches?
27. What is the rate of moisture created at varying gravel depths and heat intensity?
28. What are the effects of varying sand levels to the development of crops or the retention of water?
29. How do natural nitrogen fixing elements react to the biology of gravel gardening?

Gravel Education K-12 Experiments

Session Overview

- 20-minute presentation on projector to give an overview of what gravel gardening is
- 30-minute Cup of Gravel planting and labeling
- See following pages on the evolution of select seeds in cups of gravel

Pre-Experiment Setup Elements:

- 1 – 50-pound bag of gravel
- 1 – 50-pound bag sand
- 45 cups
- 45 Styrofoam bowls
- Seeds (Micro greens, wheatgrass and beans)
- 2 large bins to serve as big drip trays
- Labels
- Markers
- Scissors

Experiment Steps

1. Simply puncture a hole in the bottom of the plastic cup
2. Fill ¼ of the cup with sand and then gravel to the top
3. Pour small seeds on top to fall through the cracks
4. Place large seeds in the center of the gravel
5. Water to the top and let the water drip into a drip tray
6. Refill water when drip tray is dry
7. Take home after a few weeks and transplant to soil

Geological Agriculture – Lesson Plan Notes

Classroom Seed Types

The sprouting and microgreens do particularly well in indoor gravel grow cups. The recommended brand being Botanical Interests sold at Ace Hardware. Bean and pea seeds will mature to full harvest indoors, but most garden variety seeds will do best outdoors.

Monitoring

Student teams should monitor and test the configuration three times a week (Monday, Wednesday, Fri)day with moisture meters, ph meters, as well as visual inspections for height, color and overall health. If possible periodic water testing and nutrient testing is recommended. Student teams should chart results and track for the rest of the school year or through a growth cycle.

Additional Considerations

1. Students should read the manual prior to starting experiments.
2. If experimenting indoors, be sure to use containers that drain well. Also, assess sand dampness regularly. Indoors, the sand tends to dry out quicker than when using gravel gardening techniques outdoors. We recommend using clear containers when indoors to better see what is happening with the roots and moisture in the gravel system (see photos of sample planting experiments).
3. Always be mindful of depth. If it is too shallow heat can burn up the vegetation and if it is too deep the shoots may not make it to the top or the water may not make it to the roots.
4. Never experiment on cement. Heat will turn the cement into an oven and cook the rock and sand from beneath.
5. Feel free to run the same experiments using different seeds, gravel types, gravel depths, etc.
6. Email all results to gravelschool@tosoilless.com. We will feature your results in an upcoming annual report.

Gravel grow cups have several nuances for teachers to consider.

The Rules – The rules of gardening are different with gravel then with soil. Review the current edition and download at www.tosoilless.com .

Sustainable – Teachers and students can empty the cups after a plant has grown to full term and start over. The gravel will leach out plant food for over 50 years.

Classroom snacks – Through the winter, students can grow a variety of edible micro greens and sprouts on the classroom windowsill. Kids can have healthy snacks through the winter every day in class.

Take home gifts – Teachers can have students create gravel garden grow cups in class and take them home after they grow about a foot high if beans are planted.

Cups – Clear cups are better for side viewing the gravel gardening process, but a variety of cups are possible.

Outdoors – In the fall, some schools with outdoor gravel gardens do annual bulb planting with the students.

Research – Decades of research will be needed before all is known about the full range of benefits from geological agriculture practices. We invite all teachers to pick a crop type and examine it deeper against the gravel backdrop. www.tosoilless.com

Gravel Gardening Gallery 2018

Gravel Gardening Gallery

Sunflower

Tulips

Tulips

Tulips

Gravel Gardening Gallery

Nutrition Garden

Micro-Lettuce

old man and the pea

Wall of Peas in a 20 year old gravel garden.

pea high

Pea Forest in a 20 year old gravel garden.

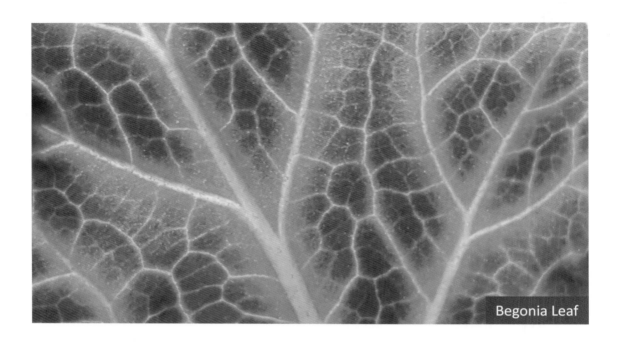

Begonia Leaf

Jade

Gravel Gardening Gallery

Lettuce

Onion Bloom

Asiatic Lily

Tomatoes

Tomatoes

Gravel Gardening Gallery

Tomatoes and Squash

Mr. Veggie

Rose

Zinnia

Zinnia

Squash

Squash

Gravel Gardening Gallery

Lima Beans

Corn, Beans, Cucumber at School Gravel Garden

Calla Lily

Calla Lily

Iris

Gravel Gardening Gallery

Sunflower

Sunflower

Gravel Gardening Gallery

Beans

Lettuce

Tomatoes

Three Types of Beans

In-Ground Gravel Garden

Gravel Gardening Gallery

Beans and Lettuce

Micro-Lettuce

Gravel Gardening Gallery

Tulips

Tulips

Gladiolus

Gravel Gardening Gallery

Basement Micro Farm Day 1

Basement Micro Farm Day 21

12 Pack of Green

Reggie

Reggie

Gravel Gardening Gallery

Closet Micro Farm

Edibles

String Beans

String Beans

Peas

Peas

On the package in soil, pea shoots grow about 2 to 3 inches in 10 to 20 days. In gravel, after 14 days they are about 14 inches.

MICRO GREENS
Peas for Shoots
Pisum sativum

USDA ORGANIC

10-20 DAYS
Sow indoors
any time of year

HEIRLOOM
Prized in Asian cuisine, pea shoots are now showing up in markets and restaurants. Exceptionally tender, shoots impart the sweet taste of fresh peas into many fresh and cooked dishes. Excellent for juicing and added to smoothies.

Botanical
I N T E R E S T S ®

Pea Shoots

Glossary of Terms

Active Layer – The active layer of a gravel garden is the 1- to 2-inch layer of the gravel garden where root development is occurring and sustaining. This layer touches the bottom of the gravel garden on top of the capillary fabric and goes up a few inches until the dry layer. Within the active layer, moisture is in contact with the gravel to activate the natural chemical action to leach materials out of the rocks for use by seeds and root systems. It is within the active layer where the ecosystem of a gravel garden sustains and feeds root systems.

Aged Gravel – Gravel that has produced crops for a full season, where the vines and leaves of the crops decay and compost back into the gravel bed, enriching or aging the gravel with a new layer of organic material. Each year of crop production in gravel will lead to a new layer of organic material being added to the gravel bed. Enriched gravel is stated in number of years that the gravel has been producing crops. It is also referred to as appreciated gravel.

Dry Layer – The top ½ inch of a gravel garden that usually stays dry or hot under the sun. This layer serves as an insulation layer to the active layer, but typically stays dry itself. Referred to as the "exposed layer," this layers looks dry in appearance compared to the active layer, which appears moist.

Geological Agriculture – The study of using rocks to grow crops without soil and fertilizer. It is also referred to as "geo-agriculture," "geo-ag" or "gravel gardening." This science combines geology and agriculture, where rocks replace soil in the cultivation and sustainment of plants and other vegetation.

Gravel Composting – The process of leaves and vines decaying on and into a gravel garden where worms and other natural enzymes interact with organic substances to compost natural materials. With gravel gardens, composting naturally occurs as each fallen leaf quickly decays on the rocks under the sun and rain. Gravel composts some vegetables where they will reseed themselves. A cherry tomato can be thrown on a gravel garden and it will compost and return the next or same season as a tomato plant.

Gravel Ecosystem – The ecosystem of the gravel growing environment is inclusive of the organic cycle between the roots, gravel, water, sand and other organic materials such as leaves and pollen. Generally speaking the ecosystem is constantly expanding as long as moisture impacts the gravel, affecting root expansion. A relatively closed ecosystem such as a gravel grow cup can accumulate decay faster than an outdoor open gravel ecosystem.

Gravel Fertility – The natural capability of rocks to sustain plant life. There are over a thousand types of sedimentary rock on Earth, each with a different level of fertility in the ability to cultivate and sustain plant development. Sedimentary rock that produces consistent crops year after year is said to have good gravel fertility.

Glossary of Terms

Gravel Grafting Theory – Gravel grafting is the theory that when you plant certain seeds in gravel, as they germinate, they also graft together to form a larger-than-normal plant heart to yield a larger-than-normal plant with greater yields. Should many seed be planted and one or a few large stalk or shoots emerge instead of many plants, than gravel grafting is said to have occurred.

Gravel Grow Cup – Small clear cups filled with sand and rock used to test seed development against a given gravel and seed type. Cup O Gravel is intended for testing and seedling development indoors. Cup O Gravel is not intended for outdoor use, nor is it intended for full-term growth except for sprouting seeds.

Gravel Juicing – The process of adding generous amounts of seeds of a variety of crops to a gravel garden to get things going well. Until the gravel garden produces as intended, gravel juicing allows you to discover what does and does not work.

Gravel Micro-Farming – A gravel micro-farm is an indoor gravel growing area of a variety of plants indoors in a basement, closet or on a table.

Gravel Moisture – The natural condensation that builds up on gravel in high heat. On hot days, gravel insulates the top inch of a gravel bed. Beneath the inch, the gravel begins to sweat in high heat, creating a degree of moisture that is capable of activating the germination process.

Gravel Water – Water that is seeped in gravel for a period of time and then drained for use in soil or elsewhere is considered gravel water. With river rock leaching nutrients into the water, gravel water is naturally fertilized water through sedimentary materials.

Nutrition Intervention – The use of gravel grow cups and other portable gravel growing environments to provide quick nutrition to populations that lack quality nutrition access.

Sand Irrigation System (SIS) – The sand irrigation system is a method of irrigation that uses sand as a water storage reservoir. The sand is set atop of plastic in the trench to retain moisture in a gravel garden. The SIS keeps the underbelly of the gravel garden cool and moist for long periods of time, allowing moisture to constantly impact the gravel to activate the leaching from the rocks.

To Soil Less

The content of this book was created and authored by:

Richard Campbell
Founder
To Soil Less™
Washington, DC
Richard@tosoilless.com

Website:
www.tosoilless.com

Follow us on our social media pages
www.twitter.com/tosoilless
www.facebook.com/tosoilless
www.Instagram.com/tosoilless

About To Soil Less™ – To Soil Less™ – A private family company based in Washington, DC, was created in 2011 for the sole purpose of sharing geological agricultural methods and technology with the agriculture and gardening industries to reduce the cost of gardening and aid in food security.